Supporting drama
and imaginative play
in the early years

Supporting early learning

Series editors: Vicky Hurst and Jenefer Joseph

The focus of this series is on improving the effectiveness of early education. Policy developments come and go, and difficult decisions are often forced on those with responsibility for young children's well-being. This series aims to help with these decisions by showing how developmental approaches to early education provide a sound and positive basis for learning.

Each book recognizes that children from birth to 6 have particular developmental needs. This applies just as much to the acquisition of subject knowledge, skills and understanding as to other educational goals such as social skills, attitudes and dispositions. The importance of providing a learning environment which is carefully planned to stimulate children's own active learning is also stressed.

Throughout the series, readers are encouraged to reflect on the education being offered to young children, through revisiting developmental principles and using them to analyse their observations of children. In this way, readers can evaluate ideas about the most effective ways of educating young children and develop strategies for approaching their practice in ways that offer every child a more appropriate education.

Published and forthcoming titles:

Bernadette Duffy: *Supporting Creativity and Imagination in the Early Years*
Lesley Hendy and Lucy Toon: *Supporting Drama and Imaginative Play in the Early Years*
Vicky Hurst and Jenefer Joseph: *Supporting Early Learning: The Way Forward*
Linda Pound: *Supporting Mathematical Development in the Early Years*
Iram Siraj-Blatchford and Priscilla Clarke: *Supporting Identity, Diversity and Language in the Early Years*
John Siraj-Blatchford and Iain MacLeod-Brudenell: *Supporting Science, Design and Technology in the Early Years*
John Siraj-Blatchford and David Whitebread: *Supporting Information and Communications Technology Education in the Early Years*
Marian Whitehead: *Supporting Language and Literacy Development in the Early Years*

● ● ● # Supporting drama and imaginative play in the early years

Lesley Hendy
Lucy Toon

372
HEN

Open University Press
Buckingham • Philadelphia

Open University Press
Celtic Court
22 Ballmoor
Buckingham
MK18 1XW

email: enquiries@openup.co.uk
world wide web: www.openup.co.uk

and
325 Chestnut Street
Philadelphia, PA 19106, USA

First Published 2001
Reprinted 2011

A catalogue record of this book is available from the British Library

ISBN   0 335 20665 4 (pb)   0 335 20666 2 (hb)

Library of Congress Cataloging-in-Publication Data
Hendy, Lesley.
   Supporting drama and imaginative play in the early years/Lesley Hendy and Lucy Toon.
      p.   cm. – (Supporting early learning)
   Includes bibliographical references and index.
   ISBN 0-335-20666-2 – ISBN 0-335-20665-4 (pbk.)
      1. Drama in education.   2. Play.   I. Toon, Lucy.   II. Title.   III. Series.
PN3171.H345   2001
372.66–dc21   2001021954

Typeset by Type Study, Scarborough
Printed and bound in Great Britain by
CPI Antony Rowe, Chippenham, Wiltshire

Contents

Series editors' preface

This book is one of a series which will be of interest to all those concerned with the care and education of children from birth to 6 years old – childminders, teachers and other professionals in schools, those who work in playgroups, private and community nurseries and similar institutions; governors, providers and managers. We also speak to parents and carers, whose involvement is probably the most influential of all for children's learning and development.

Our focus is on improving the effectiveness of early education. Policy developments come and go, and difficult decisions are often forced on all those with responsibility for young children's well-being. We aim to help with these decisions by showing how developmental approaches to young children's education not only accord with our fundamental educational principles, but provide a positive and sound basis for learning.

Each book recognizes and demonstrates that children from birth to 6 years old have particular developmental learning needs, and that all those providing care and education for them would be wise to approach their work developmentally. This applies just as much to the acquisition of subject knowledge, skills and understanding, as to other educational goals such as social skills, attitudes and dispositions. In this series, there are several volumes with a subject-based focus, and the main aim is to show how that can be introduced to young children within the framework of an integrated and developmentally appropriate curriculum, without losing its integrity as an area of knowledge in its own right. We also stress the importance of providing a learning environment which is carefully planned for children's own active learning. The present volume shows how important drama, role play and dramatic play are across the whole curriculum. They stimulate the development of the imagination, and generally help children to understand and appreciate their cultural heritage and lifestyles. Moreover, the authors show us how practitioners themselves can gain from and enjoy the whole process of being involved in drama activities.

Access for all children is fundamental to the provision of educational opportunity. We are concerned to emphasize anti-discriminatory approaches throughout, as well as the importance of recognizing that meeting special educational needs must be an integral purpose of curriculum development and planning. We see the role of play in learning as a central one, and one which also relates to all-round emotional, social and physical development. Play, along with other forms of active learning, is normally a natural point of access to the curriculum for each child at his or her particular stage and level of understanding. It is therefore an essential force in making equal opportunities in learning, intrinsic as it is to all areas of development. We believe that these two aspects, play and equal opportunities, are so important that we not only highlight them in each volume in this series, but we also include separate volumes on them as well.

Throughout this series, we encourage readers to reflect on the education being offered to young children, by revisiting the developmental principles which most practitioners hold, and using them to analyse their observations of the children. In this way, readers can evaluate ideas about the most effective ways of educating young children, and develop strategies for approaching their practice in ways which exemplify their fundamental educational beliefs, and offer every child a more appropriate education.

The authors of each book in the series subscribe to the following set of principles for a developmental curriculum:

Principles for a developmental curriculum

- Each child is an individual and should be respected and treated as such.
- The early years are a period of development in their own right, and education of young children should be seen as a specialism with its own valid criteria of appropriate practice.
- The role of the educator of young children is to engage actively with what most concerns the child, and to support learning through these preoccupations.

- The educator has a responsibility to foster positive attitudes in children to both self and others, and to counter negative messages which children may have received.
- Each child's cultural and linguistic endowment is seen as the fundamental medium of learning.
- An anti-discriminatory approach is the basis of all respect-worthy education, and is essential as a criterion for a developmentally appropriate curriculum (DAC).
- All children should be offered equal opportunities to progress and develop, and should have equal access to good quality provision. The concepts of multiculturalism and anti-racism are intrinsic to this whole educational approach.
- Partnership with parents should be given priority as the most effective means of ensuring coherence and continuity in children's experiences, and in the curriculum offered to them.
- A democratic perspective permeates education of good quality and is the basis of transactions between people.

Vicky Hurst and Jenefer Joseph

Introduction

Drama has always been the Cinderella of the arts as far as education is concerned. In the National Curriculum, it has been made to sit, with discomfort, in English, although recently some hope has been given to drama practitioners with the introduction of 'Curriculum 2000' (DfEE/QCA 1999b). Drama activities are now given a discrete heading and in the new English orders for 'Speaking and Listening' there is a distinct drama strand. However, this is still to confine drama within English whereas engagement in 'imaginative play' has potential for the whole curriculum, both as an art form and as a teaching and learning medium.

The state of play

Play, of any kind, has not been high on the agenda in recent initiatives. *Desirable Outcomes for Children's Learning on Entering Compulsory Education* (SCAA 1996) hardly mentioned play at all; the only recommendation was for 'imaginative play' mentioned under 'Creative Development'. The DfEE review of the curriculum for under-5s in June 1998 revealed that many practitioners were unhappy about the prescriptive nature of *Desirable Outcomes*, stating that 'They focused on subjects not children, and on outcomes rather than processes, thereby appearing to devalue the process of learning. Play was not mentioned, which led to learning that becomes formal too quickly'; and further: 'outcomes in many cases have led to over-formalisation of the curriculum and the proliferation of worksheets. There has often been overemphasis on adult-led learning experiences, with the result that spontaneity and play are lost' (DfEE/QCA 2000a: 1–2).

Understanding dramatic play

We could blame the introduction of *Desirable Outcomes* and its successor, *Early Learning Goals* (DfEE/QCA 1999a) as the reason for 'imaginative play' to be undervalued, but sadly this has been the case for many years. Other than in preschool and nursery settings, there is no doubt that the move towards more formal schooling for younger children has led to the demise of role play areas. Other forms of 'pretend' activity have always been on the sidelines and there has never been strong evidence of children and adults engaging in 'fantasy play'. This is in contrast to the home, where many parents encourage this kind of play and will join in such games themselves.

However, this it not the only reason for the undervaluation of dramatic activity. Drama, possibly, causes more fear among adult workers and teachers than any other of the creative subjects. On balance, trainee teachers, for example, would rather teach music than drama. The non-specialist seems to be fearful of a variety of factors that the idea of drama can present. These include both personal and pedagogical issues and are often based on previously perceived bad encounters with drama and memories of failure. These may possibly stem from previous experiences in secondary education when, in adolescence with peer pressure at its height, young people were made to feel foolish in front of their friends. Another reason why we might find the idea of drama in education difficult is that we try and compare it to what we know of adult drama. There is a perception that to use drama the early years practitioner will have to have strong personal acting skills. However, drama in education is not trying to make children into actresses and actors any more than physical education is trying to make them into the athletes or gymnasts of the future. Using drama activities with young children puts them on the path of a creative journey and helps them to develop their social, cognitive and language skills. Drama is about our humanity in all its complexity, helping us to make sense of the world around us.

The beginnings of dramatic play

'Pretend play' is remarkable in that it is one of the first activities that can be observed in the behaviour of early childhood. The willingness to 'suspend our disbelief', a term attributed to the poet Samuel Taylor Coleridge which refers to the ability to be taken metaphorically into a fictional world, begins early. Ask any group of adults what games they played as children and without exception they reply, 'mummies and daddies', 'doctors and nurses', 'cowboys and Indians', 'shops', 'hairdressers' and so on. This ability to suspend disbelief, which we look at more fully in Chapter 1, can sometimes begin before the age of 2 and often carries on until children reach puberty, and in some instances beyond.

However, there is a tension between the classroom environment and what adults think is necessary to suspend disbelief. This has led the development of drama within early years education to become marginalized; a teaching strategy used occasionally to 'service' other subjects. Often drama is seen only as a useful device to encourage personal, social and emotional development. This is indeed a strength of its use but there is no evidence that children who are given (sometimes very powerful) experiences in a drama situation assume those roles in everyday life. The bullies who have had experience within drama of being the bullied do not necessarily change their actions in any lasting way. The drama will only give them an experience of such behaviour. The kind of behaviour modification needed for such individuals is the province of 'drama therapy' and should not be the purpose of educational drama in the ordinary early years setting.

The purpose of dramatic play

What then is the purpose of engaging children in dramatic play? If it is not going to change behaviour or attitudes in any fundamental way, why engage in it at all? This is to misunderstand this mode of 'play'. When young children engage in dramatic play they take on and manipulate identity, and not just of stylized characters – they 'play out' the ideas and characteristics of their culture and their environment. The short scenarios undertaken in the role play area, the playground or in the home, sometimes complete with actions, clothing and language, represent both shared knowledge and individual experience. Bruner (1986: 109) states:

> We know the world in different ways, from different stances, and each of the ways in which we know it produces different structures or representations, or indeed, 'realities' . . . we become increasingly adept at seeing the same set of events from multiple perspectives or stances and at entertaining the results as, so to speak, alternative possible worlds.

Children instinctively engage in drama to develop their ability to understand this perspective. All mankind shares the ability to be imaginatively creative but the education and environments in which children find themselves can increasingly cut them off from their creative selves. These quickly make them adjust to a factual, material world. It is especially important for children of minority faiths and cultures, often finding themselves in the alien environment of an early years setting or school, to be able to 'play' in their cultural understanding. They need opportunities to practise what it is like to be an adult, telling stories of their lives. These activities help them to keep in touch with their cultural heritage. Through their 'pretend' stories they are making sense of their surroundings.

Children's need for stories

There appears to be a causal link between the use of narrative and early learning and thinking (Fox 1993; Grainger 1997) and therefore early years practitioners should regard stories as a very important part of early years education. Stories should not be seen as a period of entertainment for 20 minutes at the end of the session but as an integral element of children's learning. The involvement in stories with adults gives children an aural model for the cadences and intonation of the language. Hearing language spoken aloud helps the listener to understand more fully the patterns and rhythms of the discourse. As Grainger (1997) states: 'storytelling enables not just teachers but children to actively use, experience and repeat the grammatical constructions which are part of the literary language of some stories and the repetitive oral refrains'.

Stories are the lifeblood of human existence and it is important that storytelling supports children's early lives. Bettleheim (1975: 5) reminds us: 'For story truly to hold the child's attention, it must entertain him and arouse his curiosity. But to enrich his life, it must stimulate his imagination; help to develop his intellect and clarify his emotions'.

Making up stories together in an active form is also important for children's emerging reading skills. As they embark on attempting to read for themselves young children do not always have the techniques necessary to make sense of continuous written text in their head. The slowness of processing the words does not allow them access to the more complex and powerful stories found in real books (Grainger 1997). By engaging with others and with the teacher, small children are given access to the power and structure of stories through acting out their own. Through such activity they will 'appropriate' the language used by their adult communities without automatically understanding all of the vocabulary. As Anning and Edwards (1999: 74) state:

> Appropriation is the term used to describe what learners do when they use language of their knowledge communities without necessarily understanding it in the way that more expert members do. This is often evident in imaginative role play where children assume the language and mannerisms of the role.

Children are able to practise and try out 'hard words', as a 6-year-old once described them, in the story-making situation. Through problem-solving and situation-creating events children are led to their own individual understanding of the world around them. The technique to undertake this form of dramatic activity is explained more fully in Chapter 8.

We are living in an increasingly prescriptive culture where young children are more used to passive experiences. Toys are more functional and children's own imaginative resources are often underdeveloped. Practitioners frequently comment on their children's lack of creative and imaginative ability. This is not actually the case. Children are by nature imaginative but the imagination requires nurture and encouragement. With the increasing erosion of play from early years settings, it is not surprising that children find imaginative play difficult. By undervaluing role play, dressing up and imaginative play young children are led to believe that this kind of activity is not significant. It is the pencil and paper formality of 'real' education that appears to be more important to adults.

It would appear then that children from an early age participate in fantasy play to help them make sense of the world. To do this they develop storylines or 'plots' which are often over-exaggerations of real life: 'Pretence here stands as a commentary on non-pretence' (Goldman 1998: 146). This type of play is often ignored as part of the structured learning environment within the classroom. Adults set up role play areas but seldom visit them. Pretend play is seen as a useful holding activity that will engage children without the need for adult guidance. This is to undervalue such behaviour. Pretend play has much to inform us about the children we care for and teach. It also provides an extraordinary vehicle for teaching and learning.

Documents, such as the DfEE-funded *All Our Futures* (National Advisory Committee on Creative and Cultural Education 1999: 180) identify the problem. *All our Futures* notes that 'Ofsted inspections suggest too few schools teach drama in Key Stages 1–3 and provision for drama is poor because of its low status and low levels of funding. Objectives are unclear, teachers lack confidence in teaching it, and practice varies between classes in the same school'. This would be seen as a national scandal if it applied to any named core or foundation subject. We want to make the case that by undervaluing pretend play in this way we are depriving our children of a valuable learning experience.

The purpose of this book

This book hopes to redress the balance and show early years practitioners that engaging children in drama activity is not only a natural form of behaviour for small children but also a powerful learning medium. We will show how the use of drama more than adequately addresses most of the principles for a developmental curriculum which lie at the heart of this series.

Part 1 addresses 'Understanding dramatic activity'. It examines theories from the disciplines of psychology and drama which show the importance of educational drama. We look at all aspects of the curriculum to explore the range of areas that can be affected by its engagement.

In Part 2 'Managing dramatic activity' we provide examples and ideas for using drama within the curriculum to help develop not only children's social, cognitive and language skills but also an appreciation for drama as an art form. We consider progression, assessment and evaluation to help practitioners and other adults build up their observational skills in assessing drama in early years settings.

This book is for all practitioners who are prepared to take risks so that the children in their care can benefit from powerful learning experiences.

● ● ● Part 1

Understanding dramatic activity

Education is concerned with individuals; drama with the individuality of individuals, with the uniqueness of each human essence. Indeed this is one of the reasons for its intangibility and its immeasurability.

(Way 1967: 2)

1

Dramatic play from 0–6

The suspension of disbelief

The ability to suspend belief in reality and move into a 'pretend' world while at the same time knowing that the fantasy is not real would appear on the surface to be a extraordinary attribute. Most children, however, from a very early age can distinguish between the conventions of pretend play and reality. Pretend play requires the child to act in the 'as if'; a state where one thing can stand in for another. To be able to do this a child needs to be involved in a mental act of representation. This is achieved by creating a person, an event and/or an artefact that either stands for or portrays some aspect or knowledge of the world.

Aristotle described this ability as 'metaxis', and Vygotsky as the 'dual affect'. As O'Toole (1992: 98) explains, 'Simultaneously the participant can stand in another's shoes, conscientiously feeling "This is happening to me" (the first affect), and simultaneously conscious of the form "I am making this happen" (the second affect)'. Fantasy, make-believe, pretence, call it what you will, is a modality of play. This form of activity enables children to transform themselves and their surroundings from what they are into something that they want to be. Through engaging with time and space another reality is brought to 'life'.

Early forms of dramatic behaviour

The earliest forms of play which demonstrate 'this is happening to me' and 'I am making it happen' can be observed in babies' desire to move their arms and legs, experimenting with movement and with space. This early creative experimentation of kicking, extending the fingers and hands, reaching out towards objects both seen and unseen is more than just copying. It is as if the child becomes absorbed in the feelings and sensations that such actions create. The experimentation with sound and movement could be interpreted as the first stages in the understanding of mood and climax (Slade 1954).

Play is an innate process in which children desire to engage. From their very first year children imitate the people around them and from this imitation imaginary or pretend play develops. Imitative play involves children copying or imitating. Babies may copy facial expressions. As they develop they will imitate or reconstruct events they have experienced. They might use aspects of their bedtime routine while playing with a teddy. Later, imagination will influence their play. During imaginative play children are not simply copying what they have seen, but adding their own ideas. In their imaginative world children can experience things that cannot be realized in reality.

Observation of pretend play reveals how children use it to sort out their understanding of the world and gain control over events. By studying children during pretend play, we can find out what they know about their world and what is important to them. Such play appears to be an intentional process. Children knowingly manipulate actions and events to create new worlds or confirm old ones. Early forms of play show children varying between understanding things as they are in reality and as they are in pretend play.

Theoretical views from psychology

Psychologists studying play have made a distinction between several categories of social play, identifying five types: symbolic play; role play; socio-dramatic play; thematic-fantasy play; and play with rules.

One could argue that socio-dramatic play and thematic-fantasy play are very similar but we will learn that each has its own separate thinking skills. However, all of these types of play will require some form of role play. Role play, discussed further in the following chapter, has interchangeable definitions that will not necessarily please everyone. The fluidity of the term 'role play' can be seen in the following theories.

American researchers Smilansky and Shefatya (1990) proposed that there were six developmental elements associated with 'fantasy' play. These are:

- Imitative role play: child assumes a make-believe role and uses imitative action and/or verbalization.
- Make-believe with regard to toys: materials or toys are moved and used as characters.
- Verbal make-believe with regard to actions and situations: use of narration as substitute for actions and situations.
- Persistence in role play: a period of at least ten minutes is spent in developing role play.
- Interaction: at least two children play together within the context of the story.
- Verbal communication: there is dialogue related to the play.

Greta Fein (1984), another North American psychologist, carried out a series of studies in which she linked the affect of socio-dramatic play with a child's acquisition of social perspective-taking skills and self-development. By using video to capture children's play sequences, she was able to describe four levels in the development of young children's perspective-taking skills. Her research showed that between the ages of 2 and 4 years there is an increase in the complexity of children's fantasy play. Through their role taking, children are able to try out the attitudes and perspectives of others. Fein described her four levels of development as follows:

- *Level 1:* self in pretend activities – children are themselves within 'pretend' activities, e.g. 'I am pretending to teach my dolls'.
- *Level 2:* generic role transformation – child takes on the role of another in a pretend situation, e.g. 'I am a doctor looking after my patients'.
- *Level 3:* generic role with complementary – child takes on a role which involves interacting with a complementary other, e.g. 'I am pretending to be mother and I am talking to my child'.
- *Level 4:* generic role with complementary and reversibility – child can switch from pretending to be the mother talking to her child to the child answering and vice versa.

In their longitudinal study of 40 first-born children, Dunn and Kendrick (1982) also discovered that role-taking games were a common feature from an early age. They found role-taking games such as 'hide-and-seek, chaser-chased, and peekaboo were frequent features of the interaction not only between the mother and infant, but between sibling and infant' (p. 135). They found there was agreement with Bruner's four features of playful interaction in the development of language (Dunn and Kendrick 1982: 136):

- In playful exchanges the semantic domain and structure of the routine are highly restricted and well understood by the child.
- The *role structure* [emphasis added] is reversible.
- The play routines ('tasks') are amenable to having constituents varied, and the variations can be marked by vocalizations.
- The playful atmosphere of such interactions permits the child to 'distance' him/herself, in a way that sustains the child's readiness to innovate without making mistakes.

The observers recorded numerous occasions when siblings engaged in pretend play that contained fantasy or make-believe. This ability to share in pretend play was noted in children as young as 18 months.

Two modes of thinking

At this point it is important to make a distinction between socio-dramatic play and thematic-fantasy play. Whereas socio-dramatic play involves pretend activities such as laying the table, putting dolly to bed or cooking on the pretend oven, thematic-fantasy play consists of imaginary scenarios and fictional narratives. During thematic-fantasy play children create imaginary worlds for themselves and their toys based on the plots of stories they know, what they have watched on television, films they have seen or from their own imaginations.

Two American psychologists, Dorothy and Jerome Singer (1990), carried out a study into pretend play and the development of children's imaginations and found that there may be a link between two modes of thinking. Bruner (1986), who first described these two forms of thinking, defined them as the 'paradigmatic mode' and the 'narrative mode'. He explained paradigmatic thought as being involved with logic, sequencing and the ability to be analytical.

Narrative thinking, on the other hand, is more creative and requires the construction of real or imagined events. The role play area would appear to be encouraging socio-dramatic play whereas the more complex activity of interactive story-making requires children to engage in thematic-fantasy play, although this distinction may not be as clear-cut as first appears. However, it could be said that for the development of language skills and creative imagination, thematic-fantasy play is more important than socio-dramatic play. Nonetheless, it is essential that children are encouraged in both these kinds of activity in the classroom.

Theoretical views from drama practitioners

Drama practitioners have also been engaged in categorizing the development of children's dramatic play. There have been various attempts since the late 1950s to identify the developmental stages of dramatic play.

A 'developmental' view

One of the earliest drama practitioners to undertake this task was Peter Slade. In his seminal book *Child Drama* (1954) he proposed the idea that there might be some form of 'performance readiness' and that children would work towards this state through what he called 'personal' and 'projected' play. In personal play the child would engage their whole body in the activity. As Slade (1954: 27) observes: 'Personal Play is obvious Drama; the whole Person or Self is used. It is typified by movement and characterisation'.

Projected play, on the other hand, uses objects, or 'treasures or properties' as Slade refers to them, and the child, who often does not move, seems to be absorbed in extreme concentration. Here the child uses the object to 'play out' a scene: dolls, cars, Action Men, etc. take on the role projected onto them by the child's imagination. This projection onto objects develops into personal role play. At this stage the objects become extensions of the role, not the role itself. Slade's observations were very similar to those of later psychologists.

An abbreviation of Slade's developmental stages is as follows:
0–5 years:

- elementary testing stage;
- experimentation with dance and rhythm (personal play);
- the beginnings of social awareness and sharing;
- growing understanding of mood and climax;
- the beginnings of game;
- growing quality of absorption, quietness and physical stillness (projected play).

5–7 years:

- growing understanding that movement is a language;
- speech-by-movement (use of the circle and spiral appears); art forms (including less obvious music and drama);
- the game continues;
- dramatic play proper and rhythm established (circle continues but properties abandoned);
- the development of seriousness.

According to Sue Jennings (1999), a play and drama therapist, the movement from projective playing with 'things' to dramatic playing through roles and characters indicates a child's development of a conscience and an understanding of the outcomes of their actions. This comes at the same stage as the ability to talk to a toy and then reverse roles to become the toy. Jennings defined her own 'early markers of life stages' as:

- Embodiment: the physicality of play is predominant.
- Projection: the exploration of self in relation to other objects, especially toys.
- Roles: the taking on of role personally, not through toys or other objects.

Jennings' 'embodiment' play deals with the child's first experience of the world through looking, hearing, touching, smelling and feeling. It is from these first experiences that we gain a sense of self and our place in the physical world. By revisiting – as children do – these early experiences from time to time, sensory memories and forgotten ideas can be released.

Projective or symbolic play moves the child from the purely sensory into a pretend world. Here the child transforms everyday objects into other things from the 'real' world: a cardboard box becomes a boat, a chair becomes a bus and under the table becomes a house. Through replacing an object that exists at that moment with one that is absent the child is led into the notion of 'as if' – one object works 'as if' it were another. From this concept children become aware that objects can be given meaning – what Vygotsky referred to as 'reality perception' – and that the physical world has sense and significance.

Role play, as we have already discussed, is the extension of projected play. The player now takes on the role of another and plays 'as if' they were another. During this type of play children seem to perform what they already know. They will play the same scenario repeatedly, either by themselves or with others. It would appear that once freed from the constraints of the 'real' world, children are able to try out different combinations of behaviour. This type of play is characterized by the kinds of role children use.

There appear to be at least three discrete functions that roles satisfy: action, stereotypical character and fictional character. Children will engage in action play (driving a car, shopping, eating a meal etc.) where the human quality of the actor does not matter. When children have moved into stereotypical character play, we begin to see people as occupations: the builder, the policeman, the teacher etc.; whereas fictional characters take on names and some personality: the Big Bad Wolf, Jack and the Giant, television characters, etc.

These theories of 'dramatic' development take the view that the growth of understanding is a natural evolution from one stage to another. They are not advocating a structured training model.

'Play tutoring'

There have been several attempts to accelerate the development of children's dramatic play by using forms of 'play tutoring'. Brian Way (1967), a contemporary of Peter Slade, suggested the idea that dramatic understanding was developed through the seven 'facets of personality': concentration; the senses; imagination; physical self; speech; emotion; and intellect. This was described as a circle with 'the person' at its centre. Way was convinced that although there may be a difference in detail at each point of the circle, all people have these points and the potential to develop them. He saw play as an instinctive need of all people and his theory was based on the development of the individual through experience. Its emphasis was child-centred and private, and consisted of activity outside adult judgement of what was 'good' drama. Way rejected the influence of adult theatre and focused on the essential element of development in children – their ability to play.

Way's theory developed into the practice of a series of developmental exercises devised for infants through to secondary pupils. His book *Development through Drama* was the handbook for these exercises and became widely used. Way's theories would accord well with the goal notion of the new early years curriculum currently advocated, as he believed that children should move towards more complex activity the older they became.

The idea of play tutoring was also used by Smilansky (1968). Wagner (1998: 42) suggests that the idea for Smilansky's teaching of 'basic techniques' and 'the training of teachers' to intervene came from her discovery that 'children in extreme poverty do not engage in socio-dramatic play'. Smilansky's thesis that socio-dramatic play was an important influence on children's social, cognitive and language skills led her to develop several methods for increasing the amount and complexity of socio-dramatic play.

A four-variant method was devised by Smilansky and others that comprised:

- *Modelling*, in which a teacher or adult joined in the play, and which demonstrated to children how certain roles could be undertaken.
- *Verbal guidance*, which allowed 'side-coaching' where the adult would make comments and suggestions to help children develop their chosen roles but which would not become part of the drama.
- *Thematic-fantasy training*, in which children were encouraged to 'act out'

well-known fairy stories and which gave the teacher a more structured procedure to follow, as the plot was known to all.
- *Imaginative play training*, in which children were given training in techniques which developed their make-believe skills. For example, children were encouraged to use puppets, or to practise facial expressions to present different emotions.

Other researchers replicated the training using a control group to discover whether such coaching is of benefit. It was clear that there was an improvement in the quality of the play among the coached groups, but it is inconclusive whether it was the increase in socio-dramatic play or the increased involvement of adults that brought about the enhancement in learning (Sylva *et al.* 1980; Smith *et al.* 1981).

Interestingly, the term 'structured' (or 'well-planned') play was used in *Early Learning Goals* (DfEE/QCA 1999a: 10) as the essence of good play: 'Well-planned play, both indoors and outdoors, is a key way in which young children learn with enjoyment and challenge'. This would appear to indicate that the outcomes of play activity are predetermined. Although we would see dramatic play as structured, this would only apply to the process undertaken and not to the outcomes to be achieved.

Dramatic play in non-western culture

Both the observations of western psychologists and drama practitioners point to very strong evidence that there is a natural development in children's fantasy play. This is not just confined to western cultures – play of this kind is found around the world. A study of symbolic play among Turkish preschool children found that such play had an influence on the emotional, social and cognitive development of children at preschool level. Muzeyyen Sevinc's research (1999) indicated that symbolic play was instrumental in increasing children's capacity to focus on perceptual information and representational experience. Her preliminary findings showed a change in the degree of complexity and content of actions and utterances as children developed. She also found that symbolic play was an important means of helping children express their emotions and internalize social values and behaviour.

Curry and Arnaud (1984) compared the play of children in five different North American indigenous cultures. Their study indicated some common themes acted out by children in all five cultures. These included domestic play (especially based on food and feeding), family relationships, the use of toys to represent physical and human environments, medical scenarios and play involving aggressive and frightening happenings. Such socio-dramatic play can be observed in most classrooms and playgrounds worldwide.

The work of Australian social anthropologist L.R. Goldman is of special interest to drama practitioners. His study of the Huli children of Papua New Guinea shows that 'pretend' is a very strong feature of their play. He suggests that children 'play society' through their symbolic behaviour (Goldman 1998: 146). His study of children from Melanesia analyses the kinds of identity and role taken by the children in their play. He discovered that the imaginative routines of these children are heavily influenced by the strong adult tradition of the oral storytelling of myths, folk tales and legends.

The children seem to create their fantasy play on two levels: first as a 'role player' and second as 'myth-maker'. In this culture there seems to be strong evidence of socio-dramatic play and thematic-fantasy play becoming intertwined, indicating the simultaneous application of both paradigmatic and narrative thinking. Western culture does not have a strong oral storytelling tradition and this could account for the fragmentation of the different kinds of fantasy play observed in our children.

Pretend play as a natural phenomenon

The theories and research projects given as examples in this chapter make it clear that we are dealing with a very strong natural phenomenon. This occurrence is not confined only to the affluent western cultures but is present in children's behaviour throughout the world. It has become startlingly clear that 'pretend' activity is a natural and innate behaviour. In the adult world this form of 'playing society' (Furth and Kane 1992; Goldman 1998) will take place within the confines of a theatre or other purpose-built space. Here, special adults, called actors, perform pre-scripted texts and the spectators to the fiction sit in an environment of silence and darkness. The watching of television also requires an atmosphere of quietness and passivity.

By contrast, settings in which children work together are neither dark nor silent, and we must require our children to be *active participants* in the make-believe, not just passive audiences. It is essential that practitioners working in early years environments seriously consider the importance of children engaging in all types of fantasy play. Studies have shown that between the ages of 2 and 4, pretend play grows in complexity as children develop their roles and perspectives. It is unclear whether we can make the case for a causal relationship between socio-dramatic or thematic-fantasy play experience and the increase in children's social and emotional skills. However, there appears to be a strong link between the ability to develop perspective-taking skills and the development of self and social competence.

Observing children at play

There is no doubt that watching children engaged in socio-dramatic play can tell us much about their emotional well-being. In the safety of pretend play, children will let us witness their fears and anxieties. Through engagement in thematic fantasy play, we have an even more powerful medium. By working with stories developed by children (interactive story-making), we help develop creative thinking and an understanding of emotional tensions and themes. We also allow children to understand the relationships of power, status and cultural rituals within their society. All types of fantasy play promote language and communication skills and appear to be important in the development of gender and cultural identity.

The development of pretend play – a word of caution

Booth (1994) warns that the transition from children's pretend play into the more adventurous thematic-fantasy play should be approached carefully. He relates how his 4-year-old son moved from his more cautious and structured versions of fairy tales, where he wanted the adult to 'stick to the story', into his ability to improvise for himself. He explains, 'only when he entered kindergarden did he begin to allow "what if . . ." to creep into the play' (p. 24). As with other areas of development in young children, we need to be watchful and only introduce more adventurous approaches when we feel the children are ready.

Conclusion

Children need 'pretend' play not as a treat but as a right. We need to think carefully as to how good quality pretend play activities can be introduced into the classroom. We are required to meet the needs of all our children. When working with young children, we must be observant and mindful of careful intervention so that children can make sense of their different worlds in a secure and safe environment.

Summary

This chapter has examined:

- the innate qualities of pretend play;
- the theories of psychologists and drama practitioners;
- the world view;
- the difference in thinking skills required for different aspects of pretend play.

2

Understanding the 'pretend self'

We are all familiar with the 'roles' we play in our everyday lives. We can be mothers, fathers, nursery assistants, adult helpers, teachers, sons, daughters, wives, husbands, friends etc., all of which require us to take on different dispositions. Our role as practitioners requires a degree of professionalism that we do not need in our private lives. This prevents us from becoming over-friendly with our classes or their parents. The manager or headteacher will have a different relationship with their colleagues than if they were a junior member of staff. These roles, of course, are firmly based in reality and we do not rehearse them. However, by the use of a pretend medium we have the security of the 'as if' situation to sample other personalities. By 'playing out' situations that are beyond our real-life experience, we find out more about ourselves.

Following the work of American psychodramatist J.L. Moreno (1953), role play has become a very strong feature of management courses, giving participants practice in trying out different behaviours before they are experienced in real life. Simulations, an activity where circumstances and events are set up in a 'pretend' environment, are typically the vehicle used to 'play out' these roles. The adult players are often given parts to play that are above their own real-life level – e.g., the middle manager playing the managing director. Socio-dramatic play undertaken by small children in role play areas could, in some circumstances, be likened to this kind of adult activity.

The roles of children

Preschool children are still struggling to discover their own identity in real life and are in the process of finding out who they are. They will try out roles, protected by the safety of the 'make-believe' situation (sometimes complete with costume), to make some sense of their identity and their responsibilities. Parker-Rees (1999: 68) suggests that:

> When children dress up they retain their freedom to choose how they will interpret the branch-work of social expectations represented by the clothes and props they choose to use. They per-form in the sense that they dress up in the structure of the role, expressing themselves *through* the forms they choose to interpret.

Early role play in the home

The roles children assume are frequently offered to an audience. Toddlers, sometimes as young as 12 months, will 'perform' their roles for adults almost as if they are trying to gauge reaction. Parents should encourage this behaviour as it reveals that the child has reached the stage of using pretend as a means of making sense of the world. At about the same time (12–18 months) the play is enhanced by the use of objects. A cardboard box becomes a car, a blanket thrown over a table becomes a cave or tent. Everyday articles are transformed and 'children may portray events they themselves have experienced and represent situations that have, presumably, some importance to them' (Garvey 1977: 57).

Garvey also reminds us of the importance of such play. At a stage when early language is immature, parents and carers observing children's play with objects and soft toys can make assessments about the nature of the play. Garvey (1977: 59) suggests that this form of play is a significant means of communication that 'can be used to learn from the child what he is not able to convey directly or succinctly in conversations or interviews with an adult'.

As players, children assign themselves roles within the fiction. They reveal in their play not just social types but schematic frames, representing actualized everyday situations within which those roles can function. Children accept and participate in pretend play from an early age. This would suggest that they have an understanding of their 'pretend self' which appears to develop alongside their knowledge about their 'real self'. Children have a willingness to role play and in some circumstances take on characters that reveal a mature understanding of the pretend self.

The pretend self

In our view, the inconsistent and sometimes individual understandings of the terms 'role', 'role play' and 'characterization', are confusing and unhelpful. Wagner (1998: 4) describes role play as 'one of the problematic terms in this field'. We would like to propose the 'pretend self' as a more preferable term. As children enter the drama they move into a pretend self which can take on many forms and we would argue that even very young children can handle multi-role situations as they create their fictional situations.

The function of the pretend self

Children using the pretend self are not engaged in acting in the theatrical sense. Neither children nor adults are required to be actors or actresses when they take part in the early use of drama. In the context of the nursery or preschool, children will be entering into the drama primarily as themselves. They become engaged in the 'fictional' events and react to situations that are very different from their own lives. Adults help children to use their experiences to explore alternatives and look more closely at life's dilemmas and tensions. As Bolton (1984: 101) observes: 'what is required of children in drama (or at least, in the dramatic playing mode) is they be themselves, functioning in whatever way the situation demands of them'.

Pretend play could be described as children engaging with a series of different behaviours and events. It is about trying out ideas, motivations and reactions to events in make-believe situations: 'The idea of role play, in its simplest form, is that of asking someone to imagine that they are either themselves or another person in a particular situation' (Van Ments 1994: 16). It is not the skill of acting or performing in the artistic sense but that of functioning, sometimes in a more mature manner, within the fictional situation that allows growth of ideas and perceptions. Vygotsky (1978: 102) had identified this behaviour when he observed children. During play, young children seemed to reach a level in their performance that was in advance of their own developmental stage: 'In play a child behaves beyond his average age, above his daily behaviour; in play it is as though he were a head taller than himself'.

Examples of the pretend self

A grandmother whose 4-year-old granddaughter had just begun school related a recent example. The child asked her grandmother to play schools with her and surprised her grandmother by wanting to be the pupil not the teacher. They enacted a whole day at school with the child wanting the grandmother to be 'strict' and exacting. The play did not include any lessons but only the transitions of the day – registers, breaktime, lunchtime and hometime. What was of interest to the grandmother was how her granddaughter had worked hard to do everything perfectly and wanted to be 'told off' if she had not done something correctly. This example shows how children need to 'live through' real-life experiences in a safe environment. The 'telling off' in this situation is only pretend, therefore the child can learn to behave in a more mature manner. From such 'pretend' situations, small children are given strong learning experiences.

Looking at Children's Learning (1997), an SCAA companion document to *Desirable Outcomes* (SCAA 1996), has four examples of the use of pretend play as exemplars of effective learning. 'Can you move back a bit, please?' illustrates children transforming a climbing frame into a fire-engine and role playing being firemen. 'Our café', 'Is the café safe and clean?' and 'Don't forget your suitcases' are also recognizable as activities arising from role play areas set up in the classroom. (It is interesting that in a document showing examples of good practice so many of the models chosen should be of 'pretend' activities.)

The following transcript shows four children, Alex, Anna, Siraj and Duncan, using a climbing frame as a fire-engine. This example was taken from 'Can you move back a bit, please?' (SCAA 1997: 70):

Alex: Look! The house is on fire. [He moved carefully along the ladder and beckoned to the other children to follow him. He slid down the slide on his back, feet first. The others copied him.]

Siraj: No room. I can jump off. Look! [He jumped off rather than joining the others.]

Anna [to Duncan]: Can you move back a bit, please? I need more room for my hose. We need to put the fire out.

The presence of an adult in socio-dramatic play

Several studies have reported that the unintrusive presence of an adult enhances pretend play (O'Connell and Bretherton 1984; Harris and Kavanaugh 1993). Where mothers have been present and have from time to time participated in the child's activities, findings from several different studies suggest that the adult intervention in a focused way enhanced play by increasing its diversity (O'Connell and Bretherton 1984). This was taking place among children as young as 28 months. There appeared to be an increase in the duration of pretend play, the amount of time spent in planning and discussion and the maturity of the pretence. However, the play is not always helped when mothers, carers or other adults initiate ideas. By introducing new ideas or asking too many intrusive questions the child's play can be disrupted.

The following observations, undertaken in a nursery class by a trainee teacher, show some of the strengths and weaknesses inherent in adult intervention. The nursery nurse had introduced a 'television' to the role play area – a cardboard box with a clear plastic screen. The purpose of the activity was for the children, aged between 3 years, 3 months and 3 years, 6 months, to use the screen for creating television programmes. The staff had provided toys and hand puppets with which to do this. Television guides and a remote control were added and chairs arranged for 'viewing'. Initially there was a large amount of adult intervention. The nursery nurse explained and demonstrated how the 'television' worked. At this stage the children tended to be passive participants, watching the programmes the adult created. After the withdrawal of the adult the children became more adventurous. They began with simple actions – just moving the puppets behind the screen. This was undertaken without dialogue and any recognizable storyline. Songs and theme tunes were introduced, generally nursery rhymes or theme tunes from favourite television programmes. As the adult involvement became less and less, the children became more creative and stories began to be played out behind the screen.

After the initial period of setting up the new role play, when the adult was in the role play area the play tended to centre on her and although some of her questioning was helpful the children became very reliant on the adult and 'on one occasion when the adult left the role play area, all the children left with her' (Hammond 2000: 4).

Small children need time to 'grow into' new ideas, especially if introduced by an adult. The description of the children's behaviour with the 'television' gives a perfect model of the creative process. They began by finding out what could be done with the new materials – i.e. moving the puppets and toys behind the screen (the investigative stage). They then moved on to exploring their ideas and introducing some structure via the use of song and tune (the exploratory stage). Finally, they moved on to the making or recording stage of producing their own material.

Adults, however well-meaning and sensitive in their interventions, can sometimes try to circumvent this process, especially in the initial stages. Anxiety to create a structured and subject-knowledge-based curriculum has often led these early stages to be interpreted as children just 'messing about' and being unproductive. By wanting the 'product' (in this case the 'television' programmes) too quickly we can damage a very fragile and necessary process.

Unsupervised socio-dramatic play

On the other hand, leaving the role play area completely unmonitored and unsupervised because teacher intervention might 'inhibit' children (Bennett *et al.* 1996) can produce some unwanted results. Toye and Prendiville (2000: 95) argue that 'The general view is that the theme corner is the most appropriate area for productive social role play. We would like to challenge this view'. Their research revealed, along with that of Bennett *et al.* (1996), that unsupervised role play areas can produce violent and anti-social behaviour. Toye and Prendiville witnessed a boy 'vacuuming the walls in an aggressive manner ... two boys simply chased each other round a "castle" and the nature of the carefully constructed area led to no play related to its form' (p. 96).

The problem here lies not so much in the lack of supervision but in the fact that adults tend to create role play areas *for* children rather than *with* them. If the children feel no ownership of the activity, they will also not understand how the adults intend them to play in it. A young teacher in his first year of teaching spent a weekend creating what he thought would be an exciting role play corner for his pupils. By Monday lunchtime the area was, in his words 'wrecked' by the children. This is a case of children not being involved with the creation of an area and therefore having no investment in it either.

Children do like to be asked by an adult to share the experience of the development of a role play area. A researcher set up a 'Three Bear's House' role play area with some 4-year-olds. The children chose the chairs from the classroom and found household items from among the playthings. They made beds by putting blankets and cushions on the floor. After a few days of non-interventionist play, the researcher entered the role play as a 'reporter' wanting a story about Goldilocks for her paper. After being given tea and cakes by the 'Three Bears' and a 'friend' (it was unclear whether this child was a bear or not) the group shared their story:

Reporter: Hello, I am from the local newspaper, *The Bear Chronicle*. I understand you have had someone come into your house without being asked?
Kelly: She was a human.
Reporter: A human! You mean she wasn't a bear?
Kelly: No, she was human.

> *Reporter:*   Can you tell me about her? Our readers would like to know what she looked like.
> *Katie:*   She had long hair.
> *Kelly:*   No, golden hair.
> *Katie:*   It can be long too.

They contradicted and confirmed each others' version of events until the 'reporter' was satisfied that she had the details she needed. She left the play area and the tea party continued. The intervention by the adult lasted about eight minutes and the play continued for another five. The adult's role in this context was as a listener and scribe. She asked very few questions but simply prompted for clarification or asked for more detail as appropriate.

The sterile play sometimes observed in role play areas can come from familiarity with the environment and equipment that has been the same for some time. It can also come from a lack of focus where children seem to get into a 'loop' of tried ideas and rituals. An observant adult should be watchful for this kind of play as it can limit experience. The sensitive use of intervention at an appropriate moment can help to move children forward.

The pretend self in socio-dramatic play vs. thematic-fantasy play

At this point we would like to return to the distinction between what Smilansky (1968) defined as socio-dramatic and thematic-fantasy play (see Figure 2.1). The use of the pretend self discussed up to this point has been about children using 'as if' to replay or live again events in their lives to make sense of them.

Pretending in thematic-fantasy play, however, draws children into the world of the imagination and creativity. In a sense, they are making stories that have not been told before. Seldom do mood, tension or climax appear in socio-dramatic play unless the children have already been given a rich experience in other forms of dramatic play. By identifying with other people in a fictional situation, children are moving into the dramatic mode. As Bolton (1999: 252) suggests, 'Identification must imply a sufficient capacity for ownership of the fiction to allow free play within both the interpretation and 'the moment of it happening'.

Pre-scripted from everyday events and conversations

	Socio-dramatic play (solitary)	Socio-dramatic play (with partner/s)	Socio-dramatic play (with adult)
Pretend self ↓ dual affect ↑ Real self	Pretend self (sometimes as more than one person – mummy and baby). Engages in typical activities, e.g. cooking, looking after baby, making tea, going to bed, etc.	Pretend self (as leader or follower). Engages in communal activities, e.g. mummies and daddies, hospitals, shopping, etc.	Pretend self (as leader or follower). Engages in communal activities, e.g. mummies and daddies, hospitals, shopping, schools, etc.
	Real self (makes comments on action out loud), e.g. I am cooking, I am changing the nappy, I am pouring tea, etc.	Real self directs and narrates for self and others, e.g. you are mummy I am daddy, you say 'Would you like some tea?', etc.	Real self directs and narrates for self and others, e.g. you be teacher I will be child, child tells you, say in a fierce voice, etc. 'Can I take the register, now?'.

Unscripted: although often based on stories, films or television programmes etc., contains a degree of individual creativity

	Thematic-fantasy play (solitary)	Thematic-fantasy play (with partner/s)	Thematic-fantasy play (with adult)
Pretend self ↓ dual affect ↑ Real self	Pretend self (sometimes as more than one person). Using toys and objects to act out stories, e.g. monsters, favourite fairy stories, television programmes etc.	Pretend self (as leader or follower). Engaging in simple/complex story-making which is sometimes unstructured. Often using props, costumes or puppets.	Pretend self (as initiator or follower). Engaging in complex story-making which is structured by adult but allows 'ownership' by participants.
	Real self moves objects and narrates, is 'playful' with ideas and content.	Real self directs and narrates for self and others, is 'playful' and allows partner to be playful with ideas and content.	Real self (as willing participant in the make-believe) makes tacit agreement to share meaning.

Figure 2.1 Functioning in the pretend self

A *taxonomy of personal engagement*

The drama practitioners Morgan and Saxton (1987) developed a useful 'categorization of identification' to help teachers recognize the various ways in which children enter the drama situation. Their five-part classification indicated the increasing complexity of taking on different roles:

1 *Dramatic playing:* being oneself in a make-believe situation.
2 *Mantle of the expert:* being oneself, but looking at the situation through special eyes.
3 *Role playing:* being in role representing an attitude or a point of view.
4 *Characterizing:* representing an individual lifestyle, which is somewhat or markedly different from the student's own.
5 *Acting:* selecting symbols, movements, gestures and voices to represent a particular individual to others. Acting can be in the form of (a) presenting and (b) performing.

Observation of children engaged in pretending can reveal some or all of these categories. The most familiar will be 'dramatic playing', sometimes referred to as 'spontaneous improvisation', where children give a variety of responses, many of which will depend on their personal experiences. The problems set by the situation allow children to explore their reactions. However, at the same time they will also be observed using the 'mantle of the expert'. When they play 'as if' and are doctors, nurses or any other familiar adult occupation, they are taking on the role of the adult or 'expert'. The children engaged in the firefighting episode mentioned earlier in this chapter were pretending to be firemen and showing what firemen do – i.e., fight fires with water hoses. They were using the 'mantle of the expert', drawing on their second-hand knowledge of fighting fires – or at least we hope they were!

When working in story situations, we the adults can create 'mantles of expertise' for the children. We can ask them to work 'as if' they are experts in flying, in catching giants, in solving problems, etc. By encouraging children to work in the role as experts we can strengthen their imaginative abilities and build confidence in their own thoughts and ideas.

This form of play is illustrated by the following transcript of six 4-year-old children, Shuli, Liza, Tom, Janine, John and Georgina who are playing in a role play corner they have constructed using chairs, cushions and jumpers. Although this would appear to be an example of socio-dramatic play, it also contains elements of thematic-fantasy play, as we will see. There is throughout this episode a sense of tension and mood created by the main player.

Shuli	[trying to organize]: You are baby.
Liza	[in role as Mum, talking to Janine and taking off her cardigan as she 'sleeps']: Pretend you didn't make a noise, yeh. [Lots of disputes over who will be the character of Mum break out. Liza wins, although Shuli very much wants to be Mum.]
Liza	[very much in control of everyone, except Shuli]: You're the cats. [She then attends to Tom, in role as her sick baby.] What's the matter, darlin'? Pretend you are dead. [With panic in her voice] Get out, all of you get out. I'll stay here and look after him. Get an ambulance, get ambulance men.
Shuli:	He's alive.
Liza:	He's not alive. [They all shake Tom.]
Janine:	Is he dead?
Liza:	I don't know. Who'll come and lift his arms up? [Janine stares in shock and horror. There is a distinct air of tension. Tom doesn't say anything throughout. Shuli tries to become involved and reaches over to Tom.]
Liza	[shouting]: Stop it. You're not changing his nappy yet, stop it. [John tries to enter the play. Liza does not leave Tom and continues to care for him.]
Janine	[to John]: You're not allowed to play.
John:	[mumbles something.]
Janine:	You'll have to ask Liza, it's her game.
John:	Well you won't come to my party. [John leaves and quickly returns to try again.]
Liza	[to John]: Pretend you're visiting us. We're in hospital right? Georgina, say to John, 'Is it a boy or a girl?' [Shuli cannot cope with Liza controlling the play and has tried desperately to compete with her.]
Shuli	[to Liza]: Miss T. wants you. [Liza leaves the play and goes to the teacher. The teacher has not asked to see her.]

From this short scenario, we can observe children engaged as 'experts' but we can also see the fragile nature of the pretence. Liza is quite happy to come out of her mother role to 'direct' the others, telling them what to be, to do and to say. This is a very familiar feature of pretend play in the early years – there seems to be little difference between the 'real' and the 'fantasy'. At this stage the ability to create completely in role is less established and characters and roles appear interchangeable. This can be observed in the following transcript where the 'real' discussions are shown in italic. Two 4-year-old boys, Joe and Henry, are engaged in retelling the story of 'Jack and the Beanstalk', complete with sound effects, using stick puppets. This is a small sample of a 20-minute exchange. The transcript begins as they argue over where to start.

Joe: *No the beanstalk . . . hey, the cow, no . . . no, no, no, the cow first. Okay, now you have the cow first, 'cause I'm going to be Jack.* Hello, hello. *Get that cow to come, yeh, I'll bring it to mother. Hey, we need mother, you have to be mother, where's the mother?*

Henry: *Yeh, yeh, yeh.*

Joe: *You're not to shout.* Not very loud. Hello, I've bought some beans.

Henry [using Mum's voice]: Jack you're so naughty I'm going to throw them out of the window. Weee. *I have to be* [inaudible] *now don't I?*

Joe: *No you have to be the mother.*

Henry: *I've already been mother, so I'm going to be . . . now. I'm going to go to the castle* [hums out loud, action-type music]. Quickly, hide before the giant gets us! Hide, hide quickly. Fe, fi, fo, fum, I smell the blood of the Englishman. I'm going to go right here and . . .

Joe: *No, you say, 'It's just your dinner'.*

Henry [in high-pitched voice]: It's just your dinner. [Back to the Giant's voice] Oh, silly me. I'll sit down, sit down. Yum, yum.

Joe: And I got the golden hen.

Henry: *It's my turn.*

Joe: I'm going down the beanstalk. Dum de dum de dum. *Next time it's your turn and my turn to be mother. Where's mother?*

Henry: *I need to be Jack next don't I?*

Joe: *No. No, we haven't finished yet.*

Henry: *Here's the golden hen, now it's my turn to be Jack.*

Joe: *No, it hasn't finished yet.*

Henry: *I know but it is my turn to be Jack.*
           [After some further out-of-role negotiation Henry finally becomes Jack.]

Henry: Look Mum, I've got some money. Money, money, money. Quickly, quickly, run down the bean.

Joe: *Can we go now?*

Henry: No. Chop down the bean, chop it down, chop it down. Weee. Ahhhhhhhh!

Joe: Chop. *Can I be the beanstalk?*

Henry: No.

Joe: *Why?*
Henry: *'Cause it's out the play now.* [Using Jack's voice] Oh Mummy,
         Mummy. [Using Mum's voice] I'm so proud [makes kissing
         sound]. *Shall we start it all over again?*
Joe: *I don't mind.*
Henry: You've got to have the cow. Come on, walk it to market, walk it to
         market. Then he met this man. Now sell the beans.

Throughout this transcript we observe Joe and Henry going in and out
of the pretend situation with great rapidity. They take on the roles of director and narrator, seemingly without breaking their concentration on the
task in hand. They reveal a strong sense of theatricality about what they
are doing, although this performance did not have or require an audience.
It would appear that these young boys were working in a 'multi-role' situation using characterization, tension, mood and climax.

True characterization and acting in the adult sense, on the other hand,
would require children to develop a unique personality for their character.
This character would require the creation of a past and a future. This form
of characterization also requires other characters within the narrative to
make comments and discuss the traits of the main protagonists: 'Dramatic
characters define themselves through their behaviours and interactions, as
well as in what is said of them by others' (O'Neill 1995: 71). This is a far
more sophisticated skill and develops at a later date. None of our
examples has shown very young children in the pretend situation discussing the behaviour of others. Their roles were external, requiring a
notion of 'as if', but without internalization of the people portrayed. Even
if they give themselves a name ('I am Fred the fireman'), children are still
role playing and not engaging in Morgan and Saxton's (1991) definition of
characterization or acting. The presence of an adult in the play, however,
can influence the 'pretend' and in many cases requires the children in their
role playing to make observations about events and the behaviour and
interactions of characters both seen and unseen.

Child-initiated thematic-fantasy play

The example of 'Jack and the Beanstalk' showed how children's play is as
much about moving in and out of role as it is about creating the story. The
significant difference between children initiating thematic-fantasy play
and working on it with adults is one of structure. To create their text children require the opportunity to develop their ideas rapidly and sometimes
in a very disjointed manner. Making individual meaning during a larger

group activity with an adult can be more difficult. Often children have to settle for a shared meaning which may not be their individual choice. During self-initiated or partner play they can explore their own ideas about roles, action and behaviour and manipulate the story to suit their understanding. There is a 'playfulness' in this form of activity that is not always present in the more structured process drama offered by an adult.

Adult participation in thematic-fantasy play

This is not to say that adult participation is unproductive. On the contrary, without the experience of story creation in larger groups, children's skills in manipulating theatrical elements would not become so sophisticated. Unlike adult intervention in socio-dramatic play that is spasmodic and intermittent, the adult has a crucial function in the development of thematic-fantasy play. Using their more mature artistic understanding the adult can help young children shape their story in an artistic way. By introducing theatrical devices such as space, tension, mood and symbolism adults can select the aspects of the story most appropriate for effective learning and achieving curricular-orientated goals. By guiding rather than leading the storyline and dialogue onto relevant issues and ideas, children's attention can be directed towards different behaviours and actions. To undertake this, adults must be willing to suspend their disbelief and join in the children's make-believe.

The key element found in all pretend play is the concept of improvisation. As with terms like role play, improvisation also suffers from an excess of meanings: 'Although the term was shared by most people interested in drama, its applications were diverse to the point of barely sustaining a common usage' (Bolton 1999: 159). Bolton was writing here about improvisation in the late 1960s but his statement is not out of place today. In the context of early years education the term 'improvisation' could be said to be children and adults pretending to be someone else, doing something else or being somewhere else. This is played out spontaneously without a script or an audience.

The function of the adult participant

This type of pretend play with its spontaneous dialogue and continuous action is unlike other forms in that it should be played out within the medium as much as possible. In other words, a rule should be established that a signal must be given if adults or children want to break the pretend and return to the real world. This 'contract' is an important feature of adult participation in thematic-fantasy play. Children, when working with an adult to produce a story, should be given a clear understanding of what will be expected from them: 'A "contract" begins to emerge which will provide a safe and familiar framework within which the children can operate' (Baldwin and Hendy 1994: 16).

To build this safe and familiar framework all participants need to trust each other and agree to be in the same action. In order to achieve this, children must want and be willing to:

• enter into the story;
• use pretend for speech, actions and situations;
• use pretend to make objects other than what they are;
• maintain the story verbally and non-verbally;
• interact and communicate with the rest of the players;
• keep to the structure and rules of the story.

Adults should:

• have a genuine desire to work using this teaching strategy;
• be prepared to enter the child's world and believe in what they are doing;
• take the children's work seriously;
• understand how improvisation functions;
• understand the learning potential of any particular story and keep this to the fore;
• be willing to take risks;
• encourage problem setting and problem solving;
• allow the group time to make decisions.

This type of adult participation will be further developed in Part 2 of this book.

Making a contract

Making a contract with the children before a drama session is a valuable way of defining or reiterating expectations. However young the children, contract making should be a joint responsibility, not something that is just imposed on them. What do the children consider as important? Do they think we should laugh at comments made by others? Do they think that it is a good idea to talk over the top of others, or support others by listening? It is worth spending time establishing and re-establishing a general agreement about how to behave throughout the drama, and if so why?

The children should generate these ideas even if the adult helps to shape them. It is vital that the children understand not only what they are agreeing to, but why. Why should we listen to others? How do we feel if we are sharing an idea and someone laughs?

This process of contract making, although specific to the drama, is developing a wider awareness of personal and social skills. If there are problems with any aspect of the contract during a drama session, it may be that subsequent sessions are used to address this issue. When children find it difficult to listen to one another you could introduce a 'circle time' *within* the drama in which everyone has a chance to speak. For example, all the animals in the wood could come together to decide how they will cross a river. Each animal has a chance to speak and the other animals are asked to listen quietly so a decision can be made.

Conclusion

Dramatic activity with children can be quite a challenge for adults. As Way (1967: 183) observed: 'this very factor of scriptlessness, which makes improvisation of such value as an activity for children, is often the major reason why many teachers dislike it'. With the increasingly prescriptive, structured and teacher-directed curriculum, such activity can be seen as lacking in clear objectives and hence too risky. This is to misunderstand the complex nature of this form of learning. By engaging children in strong 'pretend self' experiences, both in socio-dramatic and thematic-fantasy play we are providing an effective mode that can develop both cognitive and affective learning.

Summary

This chapter has examined:

- the concept of the pretend self;
- the nature and function of the pretend self in socio-dramatic play;
- the importance of 'ownership' in role play areas;
- the need for different kinds of role play area;
- the nature and function of the pretend self in thematic-fantasy play;
- the importance of sensitive adult intervention and participation.

3

Language, drama and the imagination

Children's ability to speak and to listen is fundamental to their language development, learning in school, and to social development.

(QCA 1999: 3)

With the introduction of the Literacy Hour in primary schools in September 1998, children as young as 3 have been introduced to knowledge about language in its technical sense. Nursery and reception classes in the state sector are being exposed to capitalization at the beginning of sentences, commas, full stops and the use of speech marks. Very often, the story contained in the text being used appears irrelevant and sometimes is never mentioned to the children at all. Although raising the focus on reading and writing standards is laudable, it has meant that the development of speaking and listening skills has taken a back seat. For young children who learn most effectively through doing and through talking about what they are doing, this move may be misguided.

Even in the late 1960s concern was being shown about the lack of interest in and understanding of 'oracy'. In 1965 Wilkinson indicated his concern when he wrote: 'The spoken language in England [had] been shamefully neglected; where it had been mentioned in official reports, the concepts had been puerile, distorted or misconceived. "Oracy" was as fundamental to education as literacy and numeracy. It was not a "subject" – it is a condition of learning in all subjects' (cited by Dixon 1991: 25). All cultures throughout time have had language, existing mostly in sound as a spoken and heard phenomenon. Written language is a comparatively recent invention and many languages worldwide exist only in an oral form. Of the 3000 languages found in the world today only 78 have a literature (Edmondson 1971; Ong 1987).

Young children of all cultures acquire information through active engagement with people, places and events. In these early stages it is talk with others that is made into theories, beliefs and understandings. These in time become altered by having different encounters with the world. Real-world casual knowledge is edited and updated frequently as new information is absorbed. A child will not respond, for instance, to spilling water on their favourite teddy in 'pretend' play with the reciprocal 'drying' of the bear until they know from their real-world experience that liquids when spilt make other things wet.

Early language

Children's first encounters with language are as speech. This occurs long before they understand the purpose of phonology or orthography. They can produce language in the spoken form very effectively before they are introduced to knowledge about its form and function. Early language is practised aloud. Babies make noises with their mouths and lips which are later replaced by recognized vowel and consonant sounds (Garvey 1977). 'Da-da-da' and 'ba-ba-ba' are early sounds in the repertoire. Parents become excited when recognizable 'ma', 'da' or 'pa' sounds are produced when the relevant parent comes into view. Children begin to lose their ability to distinguish the wide range of differences between speech sounds when they are about 1 year old. By the beginning of their second year, they are focusing on the sounds of their particular language and making sense of the different patterns of sound they hear.

An important advance in language seems to be made between the ages of 2 and 3. At this stage toys are often given an audible action-identifying tag such as 'baa-baa' for toy sheep, 'woof-woof' for a dog, 'moo-moo' on seeing a cow, etc. Children then use these identifiable sounds when they play – a car noise will be made as the toy car is pushed along. It would appear that from this stage children are beginning to use language for meaning.

The value of early talk

In all good early years settings where talk is a valued activity, children are given opportunities to discuss, ask questions, describe things, develop and explore ideas, demonstrate what they know and offer their viewpoint. All aspects of these talk activities are conducted in a climate where children's opinions are taken seriously and their contributions respected.

By introducing writing too soon we may be restricting language and vocabulary to a point where children will find it difficult to write anything of importance to them. A teacher, following Key Stage 1 Standard Assessment Tasks (SATs), said she felt that there was no doubt that the children had become technically very competent writers but sadly they had nothing to write *about*. As Alison Sealey (1996: 12) observes, 'A key difference from a teacher's point of view between the two modes is that while children learn to speak without formal tuition, they do not usually acquire literacy merely by being members of a literate community'. It is the methods we use to help children join the literate community that are crucial.

The importance of discursive language

Discursive language is particularly important in the growth of children's thought and understanding. Talking *through* an event or an idea can help develop perspective and meaning and at the same time build vocabulary and grammatical understanding. Evidence from cases such as Genie, an American child deprived of communication until 14 years old, helps us to understand the importance of the 'dialogic character' (Sealey 1996) of spoken language. Genie is described as having been physically punished if she made any sound and from an early age she had been kept confined away from constant contact with other humans. When she was found she was totally without language (Pinker 1994; Aitcheson 1997). She then began to learn to speak but her understanding and production of language were always at a rudimentary level.

A case personally known to us concerns a 15-year-old boy confined to a wheelchair all his life with a rare muscular disorder. He had not used spoken language until the age of 15 when he was helped, through speech therapy, to begin to say things aloud. Although he could read and write at an elementary level he never fully mastered grammatical speech.

In contrast, Aitcheson (1997) cites the case of Isabelle, a child deprived of speech. Isabelle, who had lived with her deaf-mute mother until she was found at the age of 6 and a half, could only make noises. This child, unlike the teenagers cited above, made rapid progress with her talking and made up six years of development within two. We need to be cautious of individual cases as there may be other conditions present, but what these cases do reveal is that there is a critical period for learning spoken language. Research shows that by the age of 6 this ability is on the decline (Aitcheson 1997). Learning to write rather than speak the language too early may be detrimental to young children's linguistic development'.

Talk in educational settings

Educational settings have been described as 'socio-linguistic' environments. That is to say, most children share a common language. This language will be unique and individualized to each child and yet it exists in a way that enables communication between individuals to take place. Communication in the classroom, however, can be very unlike talk in everyday circumstances; it has some recognizable features not exhibited in everyday talk situations.

The problem for education is that spoken language is flexible, unstandardized and has few conventions. Subconscious knowledge of turn taking is one of the common features in most talk situations. In settings where there are groups of children, the routine of hand raising before speaking is the norm as it allows some form of control. Although adults have the right to speak whenever they please, children are often asked to raise their hand before they can ask their questions or make their comments. Even in the freer conditions of group work the young children's talk is still frequently organized and monitored by the adult who is seen by the children to be the person with all the knowledge.

The collective nature of the language programmes required by recent governments has meant that prolonged periods of talking between adults and children or children and children no longer have a place within the pressurized curriculum. Many practitioners express regret that they can no longer afford the time to talk with their pupils on matters that are outside the curriculum. A *Dispatches* programme, 'The Early Years' on Channel 4, highlighted the problem. The accompanying booklet quoted a 1995 survey that showed that during a three-month period of two-minute observations, researchers found that out of the 300 observations 'only 10 showed spoken interaction between children or between child and adults' (Mills and Mills 1998).

The quality of language during pretend play

Corinne Hutt (Hutt *et al.* 1989) undertook research into the development of spoken language during children's fantasy play. She found that during periods of pretend play children's utterances were longer and contained a considerably higher proportion of adverbs and modal auxiliary verbs (will/shall/can/may – you *won't* come to my party) than when they were engaged in non-pretend activities. When using the pretend self children displayed a much greater linguistic competence than at other times. An Office for Standards in Education (Ofsted) survey of reception classes in

1994 reported that: 'Better overall standards in literacy were achieved where the development of spoken English is taken seriously and well-planned. When this occurred . . . drama and role play were used effectively' (Ofsted 1994).

The significance of dialogue

Increasingly the teaching strategy of 'question and answer' is used as the common discourse in many settings. With the pressure on time and the overwhelming need to evaluate what children are learning, this form of teaching method is seen as central to a good learning environment. Adults ask questions that require specific answers and some children struggle to find the correct response. By controlling the answers adults force children into a 'what is in the adult's head' game. Learning that there are 'right' answers to adults' questions takes place as early as 2 to 3 years. Children learn very quickly to be wary of these questions and many will not risk being wrong. They either will not answer at all or when prompted give a one-word or short-phrase reply. As Toye and Prendiville (2000: 90) observe, drama talk 'is not the abstracted, hypothetical, "talk-about" type of language that most classroom talk consists of, a language which is hard to become involved with the younger you are'. By relying too much on this form of discourse, a wide gap appears between the conceptual frame of children and that of adults.

The well-documented study by Tizard and Hughes (1984), comparing the conversations a group of 4-year-old girls had with their mothers and those they had with their nursery teachers, seemed to suggest that young children of all social backgrounds learned more from talking with their mothers than their teachers. A discrepancy was shown to exist between 'the richness, depth and variety' and 'the sense of intellectual struggle' (Hughes and Cousins 1991: 112) present in the home talk compared with the talk undertaken in the nursery setting. Here the children made minimal responses to (rather low-level thinking) questions put to them by adults.

To illustrate this more clearly, the following example shows the effect of adult intervention on the pretend play of some 4-year-old children in a home corner. At the beginning of the sequence they are playing by themselves without adult intervention. A nursery nurse then joins the play.

Emma: Here you go. [A cup is given by Emma to Sara.]
Sara: It's nearly time to go.
Adam: It's eleven o'clock to go.

Sara: No, it's not really eleven o'clock.
Emma: We need to cook something.
Adam: Look that's off.
Emma: It doesn't matter if they are different colours.
Adam: I'll throw the pancake in the air.
Sara: No darling! We must go shopping now.
        [At this point a nursery nurse joins the play and tries to engage the children in packing to go on holiday.]
Nurse: When mummy and daddy pack, what do they have to do?
Emma: This is how you fold.
Nurse: What do they do to shut the lid?
        [No reply.]
Nurse: Are you going to shut the lid?
Sara: We've finished.
Nurse: Is it done up?
Sara: No!
Nurse: If you were upstairs and it is morning, all these people would still be in bed. [Showing them a doll.] Are you going to get them dressed? [No reply.] Will you dress the dolls now?
Sara: Yes.
Nurse: Has that one got a nightie on?
Sara: A long nightie.
Nurse: Do you want to dress one, Emma?
Emma: No.
Adam: Where's the other?
Nurse: Which other one?
        [No reply.]

Comparing the adult intervention with the children's initial unsupervised play we find the adult contribution confirms the Tizard and Hughes' findings of 'minimal' response to 'bland' questions.

The difficulty of direct questioning is illustrated further by the experience of Michael, a nursery child who had for six months chosen to be an elective mute when he came to school. The staff were concerned that he might have retarded language skills as he did not speak much at home either. During a drama session taken by an outside drama practitioner the children became engaged in 'making toys' for Father Christmas as he and his elves all had the flu. Michael, who was 3 years, 8 months at this time, worked by himself making an aeroplane.

When it came to the time to go home, Michael suddenly spoke, inviting everyone onto his plane, complete with a bag of toys he had 'collected' to take home. He insisted on being the pilot and made sure everyone had their seatbelts fastened correctly. An adult who mimed a car seatbelt was 'told off' and asked to 'do it properly'. After the plane landed the children went back to the classroom and Michael gave everyone a 'toy', saying their name as he did so.

There was no question Michael had good language skills, but not until that drama session had he been given the freedom to use them. It later became apparent that Michael could not cope with direct questions.

Ironically, most talk outside educational settings is of a different style. Statements are made by one participant, often followed by another statement from someone else that either elaborates or explains the first statement. Direct questions are rarely used as a common form of communication. We are not suggesting that direct questions should never be used but we do ask practitioners to think carefully about the nature of the question and its purpose. Does it ask children to speculate and reflect or does it require them to give a 'right' answer?

Learning is the product of curiosity and the need to know something. The right question or helpful statement at the right time has an active role in the development of curiosity and therefore in the thinking and learning process. Work by Morgan and Saxton (1991) in *Teaching, Questioning and Learning* showed that it was more important to ask *'What do I want this question to do?'* than *'What type of question should I ask?'* They developed three categories that were much broader in range:

- *Category A: questions which elicit information.* These are questions which draw out what is already known in terms of both information and experience and which establish the appropriate procedures for the conduct of the work.
- *Category B: questions which shape understanding.* These are questions which help teachers and pupils fill in what lies between the facts and sort out, express and elaborate how they are thinking and feeling about the material.
- *Category C: questions which press for reflection.* These are questions that go beyond the facts and demand intellectual and emotional commitment by challenging the individual to think critically and creatively.

These categories were developed for use with older primary and secondary pupils. In early years education we should be aware of the effect of direct questioning that, as we have observed, can limit rather than encourage conversation. For our purposes in would be preferable to rephrase each category as 'talk' which either elicits information, shapes understanding or presses for reflection. Listening, thinking and hearing one's own answer are the three interdependent components that we should promote to deepen language skills.

By engaging children in conversation the following kind of dialogue is possible. A group of nursery children in their first term at school and their adult helpers had developed a story based on the nursery rhyme the 'Old Woman Who Went Up in a Basket'. Their adventure had taken them to the moon to find and rescue her. They had discovered the Old Woman and found a train to take her home. One of the adults took on the role of the Old Woman. The following exchange between Nigel (aged 3 years, 2 months) and the adult took place as they conveyed the Old Woman onto the train:

Nigel: We'll soon be home. It is only a little way now. [He leads the others and the adult around the area moving his arms like a train.] Here we are [stopping the train in the station].

Adult: Oh, good. I was beginning to wonder whether I was ever going to go home. It was very kind of you to come and find me.

Nigel: Oh that's all right. It was easy.

Adult: That's good. I need to tell you though, I've lost my basket and I don't know how we are going to fly off the moon without it.

Nigel: I'm a fireman, I know about very long ladders. I'll get us off the moon. Don't you worry [he pats the adult on the arm].

What is remarkable about this short dialogue is that the child involved was barely 3 years old and the story took place on his first day in nursery! You will notice how the adult helper did not ask direct questions but gave openings for the conversation to continue.

Language as a social function

Parents, carers and other workers are given an effective tool to change the management of spoken language and children's perceptions of the world when they use dramatic play to develop talking. Through exciting dramatic play, young children, with the guidance of adults, are put in control of their own speaking and listening. They become active contributors to their own learning by being given the responsibility of having the relevant knowledge for the play situation in which they are engaged.

The quality of language plays an important part in the significance of the drama experience. The strength and depth of the work is influenced by how young children control the talking and the non-verbal elements of the drama, and how they handle the shift from literal to symbolic situations.

Speaking in a make-believe situation provides a setting in which the speech can occur naturally. The talk does not remain in isolation and out of context but becomes part of the interaction of the drama. Young children are allowed to express themselves individually and as a group.

Adults are not always such good listeners and can sometimes dismiss children's contributions as being irrelevant or not to the point. We would like to suggest that children's verbal input is not random or thoughtless. If we take the time to unpack an idea by encouraging children to think through what they have said, we can often find that their train of thought is very inventive and creative. They should be asked to engage themselves not only intellectually in the narrative but emotionally as well. It is this combination that can make learning through drama so effective. The power of the medium comes from the experience of the language and the significance of dramatic events.

Language as function

In these experiences children are working out a semantic code and finding that language has a function. M.A.K. Halliday (1975), a prominent researcher in this field, identified seven categories of language function: instrumental, regulatory, interactional, heuristic, personal, imaginative and representational. Between the ages of 1 and 2 years, children begin to understand the power of the instrumental function. As soon as they utter 'I want . . .', 'I won't . . .' they recognize that language can influence other people, especially their parents.

Personal identity and the development of personal relationships become a feature as children begin to use 'heuristic' language. Halliday suggests that his own son Nigel moved into adult language at the age of 9 months. It is at this stage that children begin to ask questions about the world in which they live. We see the introduction of 'pretend' during this period, where language is used in its 'imaginative' function.

Halliday divides the personal and heuristic stages into their experiential, logical, interpersonal and textual components, which he labels 'ideational' or 'language as reflection'. As Halliday (1975: 114) observes, 'it is worth remembering that narrative develops first as a strategy for learning, and it is only when the ideational potential comes to be combined with the imaginative function (which has developed independently of it) that fictional narrative is born'.

Language, narrative and thinking skills

The two modes of thought, touched upon in Chapter 1 – the paradigmatic and the narrative – were advanced by Bruner in 1986. This was a period when there was much interest in the development of thinking and language in the linguistic community. For Bruner, the paradigmatic mode relies on making connections between ideas and events. These ideas and events verify an existing truth. He notes that young children are initially weak in this way of thinking until inducted into it through education. For example, young children have some difficulties in counting 'one-one'. They are able to count bricks accurately when they are displayed in a row but if the row is subsequently rearranged they will say there are a different number of bricks to the ones they counted. As with all good scientific thinking the 'paradigmatic' mode uses the power of observation to create conceptual frames.

The paradigms or models made by children come from their observations of their everyday lives. In their socio-dramatic play, for example, they play 'mummies and daddies' or 'doctors and nurses' based on their observations of how these groups behave. They observe doctors talking to mothers and use their observations of these dialogues in their play. In preschool and nurseries, children as young as 1–2 years play with telephones and cooking utensils, using their knowledge of adult behaviour. A recent incident given by a mother describes how her 11-month-old picked up his toy telephone and babbled into it while she was on the phone to friends.

Idealized representations

There appears to be a second stage when children's observations take on an 'idealized' form. Children develop paradigms of other worlds they do not inhabit (e.g. all teachers wear mortar boards, all doctors have white coats, all 'Eskimos' live in igloos). A version of real life exists through these shared stereotypes, expertly exploited by the writers of soap operas. The success of such programmes relies on the shared idealization of human life and in some cases can lead the viewer to believe the characters they are witnessing really do exist.

Children need a strong sense of language to explore with adults the range of images they see on television and video. Dorothy Heathcote used the shared ideas children have about their world to develop the process she called 'dropping into the universal' of human experience (see Wagner 1979). She firmly believes that through time people have found themselves in the same situations and that drama is the tool that can remind and teach children of this universal state.

Within drama, adults can use events to draw children's attention to the significance of an incident or action. In doing this they can help children to see the implications for their own lives and the lives of others. However, success relies on the use of both paradigmatic and narrative thinking, which are situated in different areas of the brain. For Heathcote, making connections between past and present knowledge and experience is the important element of thinking. Children and adults in drama must be prepared to take 'imaginative' leaps to make these connections.

Bruner (1986) distinguishes between the 'imaginative' leaps taken in paradigmatic thinking and those undertaken in the imaginative thinking of the 'narrative mode.' The synthesis of information made in 'paradigmatic' thinking creates ideas firmly based in reality, not in fiction, as is required in narrative thinking.

Narrative thinking, on the other hand, allows for inconsistency and innovation beyond literal truth. Children working in the narrative mode are quite happy to be made small by drinking magic potions, as in *Alice in Wonderland*, or to grow wings or fly on a magic carpet. However, when working in a paradigmatic mode they solve their problems through logical and world truths – for example, people cannot grow wings in real life. Bruner (1986: 11) argues that 'a good story and a well-formed argument are different natural kinds [of modes of thought]'. He cites the logical proposition of an algebraic formula and the narrative 'the king is dead, and then the queen died'. He suggests, 'One leads to a search for universal truth conditions, the other for likely connections between two events – mortal grief, suicide, foul play' (1986: 12).

Language as meaning

Sperber and Wilson (1987) forwarded the view that it is the human condition to try and make sense of everything we hear. Their 'relevance' theory explores how the hearer searches for meaning by drawing inferences from the speaker's words. Conversely, children do not speak so that they can be heard to utter beautifully grammatical sentences (contrary to some recent thinking about language teaching) but in order for someone else to understand them. How difficult it must be for the novice to make sense of much of the language that is heard in educational settings. For some children the use of story or narrative as a mode of communication becomes an important aid to their learning in these early years.

Where paradigmatic thinking searches for higher and higher degrees of abstraction, the narrative mode allows the child the chance to dream. When we are allowed to fantasize and dream we can create a narrative for our lives through our experiences. Creating narratives seems to be a natural instinct. Listen to any small child playing and they will speak aloud their actions and their thoughts as if telling a story. The story of our life changes as we gain more experience and understanding.

Storytelling is important not only as a means of searching for and making meaning in our lives but as 'a primary act of mind transferred to art from life' (Hardy 1977, cited in Grainger 1997: 34). Harold Rosen (1991: 15) suggests that 'Everyone knows we tell stories in our heads. For every one we tell to others, there are thousands which are strictly between us and our alter egos. We daydream in narrative and we dream in narrative . . . there are widespread claims that the real significance of narrative is that it is a fundamental way in which the mind works'. The use of stories in the early years should go beyond mere recall and comprehension. Stories should be offered to children as a means of exploring their creativity and imagination.

The development of the imagination

Policastro and Gardner (1999: 213) suggest that 'Imagination is a form of playful analogical thinking that draws on previous experiences, but combines them in unusual ways, generating new patterns of meaning'. Frank Smith (1992: 45) suggests that 'imagination is constantly underrated'.

Only in the realms of art or invention is any credibility found in the imagination. Other activities such as fantasizing or daydreaming are considered to be either self-indulgent or irresponsible. But we cannot help our brain being imaginative, as this is its fundamental condition. What we can develop is the use we make of our ability to be imaginative. Guilford (1958) put forward the view that to be an imaginative and creative thinker there would need to be a fluency in thinking which was linked with an ability in word fluency, the ability to link one idea to another and the ability to express ideas with ease.

Craft (2000: 41) believes that 'being imaginative is distinct from fantasy'. She indicates that several other writers have also pointed out that 'fantasy' is only combining what is already known, whereas imagination requires the world to be viewed differently in significant ways. As Craft points out, Kenny (1989) suggests imagination 'enables the thinker to form new thoughts and discover new truths and build up new worlds'. (Craft 2000: 41) This cannot be achieved without a rich experience using the spoken word.

Developing symbolic language

Wagner (1998: 25) reminds us that 'Like drawing, symbolic play is a way of saying, "This stands for that" '. Young children do this every time they use one object to stand for another – the banana that becomes a telephone, the ruler that becomes a sword, two closed fingers used as a gun. There has been research into how children are able to do this without 'representational abuse' (Leslie 1987). In other words, what is a child doing in their head that allows them to use one object in place of another without corrupting their primary conceptual knowledge? Leslie, borrowing a computer metaphor, suggests that when children are engaged in pretence, or watching others engage in pretence, they create a copy of their primary concept and perform mental changes on it. These 'copies' are then either stored or discarded, leaving the original intact.

This gives a plausible explanation for children's handling of metaphor, their ability to create a representation of an idea or event, and their ease at employing objects that carry a meaning beyond their physical presence. By engaging young children in interesting and stimulating story-making experiences we should find that there is not only a growth in confidence and independence but also a development of this kind of language. This is why the 'acting out' of a fairy story, that passes as drama in many settings, serves little purpose. To develop language and imaginative thinking fully children need to make their own stories in which metaphor and symbol become a strong feature.

The role of the drama storyteller

If listening to a story 'underpins and complements the growth of language' (Grainger 1997: 10) how much more powerful that experience will be if you can be in the story and develop it for yourself. Young children are accomplished storytellers and will instinctively follow a classic story structure. Writers on the art of storytelling, such as Propp, have observed that this structure is the most complete and satisfying. To be so it has to contain a beginning, middle and end (the climax), and to make it satisfying it must include tension (complications) and surprising events. Every writer of the popular action-film genre knows this to be so (see Figure 3.1).

Children can create a 'classic' story from as young as 3. When working with children in this way we have found that they will invariably 'put in' the first complication to add tension to the storyline. Fox (1993) supports this theory:

> She [Fox] provides clear evidence that pre-literate children with a wealth of experience of story (gained through conversation, traditional tales, nursery rhymes, books, television and so on) display a degree of knowledge about narrative convention and form, and linguistic styles

and plot which is usually associated with more mature and highly literate readers and writers.

(Grainger 1997: 35)

With the current interest in children's ability to write, an early exposure to the structure of stories and narrative patterns can only enhance their knowledge of these conventions. Storybook language is often used by

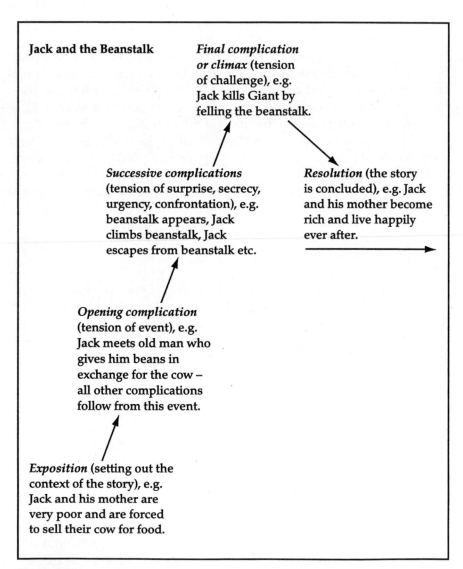

Figure 3.1

very small children engaged in story-making. For example, a group of nursery children aged between 2 years, 10 months and 3 years, 4 months invented 'golden horses' on which to ride to find the princess. Suddenly Keiran (aged 3 years, 4 months) stopped and pointed in front of her. 'Look,' she said. 'There in the trees, can you see it? That golden turret gleaming in the sunlight.' She was unaware of the power of what she had said but it must have come from a story she had heard more than once.

The importance of reflection in narrative

Young children are keen 'plot guzzlers' in their early experiments with story-making. Plot in this context is the storyline which develops the characters, their existence in time and their actions. It could be likened to the 'and then', 'and then' repetitive construct found in children's early attempts at writing a story. We suggest that this is an important stage and should not be dismissed as being irrelevant. The danger is similar to the damaging acceleration of the creative process in which children are asked to move onto the next stage too quickly. To move forward from 'plot' invention, young children need a strong 'real life' understanding of temporal and spatial events. Even in the retelling of a well-known story very young children want the possibility of changing the 'plot' to make it their own. Recently, during some work with some 4-year-olds, Samantha (aged 4 years, 5 months) was not satisfied with re-enacting what a certain character had done. She insisted that if she had been that character she would have done something completely different: 'If I was Ruby I wouldn't do that, I'd run away.' She then ran from the scene, and had to be retrieved from the toilets. Her suggestion altered the course of the entire story.

Young children need to work through this stage of plot development before they can linguistically tackle activities that ask them to 'stand aside' from the story and consider what are the consequences of actions and behaviour. The more sophisticated plot found in the dramatic form of adult plays requires the characters to make intentional decisions and choices that influence the outcome of the storyline. From our experience, this understanding of plot development should be presented to young children *very slowly*. It is not until about 4 years, 6 months that children appear to be able to work successfully with 'stand-aside' techniques. The careful introduction of drama conventions will help to encourage reflective moments.

The need for reflection

As children's need for 'plot only' recedes, it is Halliday's (1975) 'ideational potential' of narrative, the manner in which we can help children reflect on what they say and do, that provides drama practitioners with a potent learning tool. Reflection within the narrative is a very important feature of educational drama. Young children are very familiar with both visual and aural narratives from their engagement with picture books. As Nicholson (1996: 250) observes, 'Unlike the later emphasis on reading as a private, individual enterprise, when young children read picture books it is a shared and communal activity: good readers for children encourage discussion of visual narratives, and do the voices or actions'. When we engage young children in drama we can make the picture book come alive. The voices and the actions can be taken on by everybody, making children active contributors to the event.

By asking children to pause and reflect on people's ideas, actions and motives the adult can guide them in their understanding of cause and effect. Often children can engage in an action or dialogue that is detrimental or denigratory to others. At these moments the consequences of such an event can be explored either in the story or outside. Children will often use guns as a means of fending off their foes. An adult can respond by clutching their arm to show they have been shot and asking for help. Responding in role to some unkind remark can make the speaker think again about the consequence of what they have said. Unlike real life, in story-making the 'plot' can be suspended and children asked whether they would like a rerun of the last event as its consequences were not as we expected. This is a talent most of us would like to have in real life!

Reflection can provide children with ways of identifying with the universal predicaments as explored by Dorothy Heathcote. Bettleheim (1975: 11) argues that the fairy tale 'is future-orientated and guides the child – in terms he can understand in both his conscious and unconscious mind – to relinquish his infantile dependency wishes and achieve a more satisfying independent existence'.

Conclusion

Spoken language, albeit unpredictable, is the most successful mode of learning for young children. They are given experience in both paradigmatic and narrative thinking when they engage in socio-dramatic play and creative story-making. By building a strong spoken language base, children will have greater access to the later, more formalized aspects of literacy.

Summary

This chapter has examined:

- talk as both a personalized and social activity;
- educational talk and its conventions;
- talking through events as an important feature of language development;
- dialogue and its significant features;
- language, narrative and thinking skills, which are closely linked;
- imagination, which requires the thinker to view the world in different ways;
- engaging children in dramatic story-telling, which provides them with a model of story structure;
- reflection as an important aspect of the dramatic process.

Drama and personal, social and emotional development

Adult: What do you like about drama?
Daniel [aged 5]: When you tell out the things what you feel.

The wish to represent and share our experiences, feelings and desires is a basic human need. From the earliest moments of life, we find ourselves in an attachment relationship with others; our parents, our siblings, carers both inside and outside the home. If this relationship with parents or carers is damaged in any way the child feels a sense of loss and disorientation. Attachment in social development appears to be very important (Bowlby 1980) and the behaviour exhibited by children deprived of strong attachments can become a cause for concern.

There has been a recent and worrying rise in the level of difficult behaviours being presented by young children at home and in early years settings: temper tantrums, aggressive behaviour towards others, excessive tearfulness, clinging to adults etc. The difficulty for adults in the modern setting is that problem behaviours take time to manage, and time is in very short supply. Combine this with the pressure on early years practitioners to increase children's attainment levels and the tolerance of such behaviour diminishes. The judgement criteria used by adults to determine whether a child's behaviour is normal or abnormal have narrowed.

Disruptive behaviour is no longer being accommodated and there are, for the first time, instances of children as young as 5 being excluded from school. A report, compiled by the children's mental health charity Young Minds, indicates a significant increase in the number of cases of young children under 5 suffering from 'severe emotional deprivation' (Burke 2000). With further calls from government to accelerate the academic and intellectual abilities of our children, we must be careful not to allow their emotional development to be retarded. This makes a strong personal, social and emotional programme even more important for young children.

A definition of personal, social and emotional development

Curriculum Guidance for the Foundation Stage (DfEE/QCA 2000b: 28) suggests that 'this area of learning is about emotional well-being, knowing about who you are and where you fit in and feeling good about yourself'. Personal, social and emotional development covers every area of children's relationships with others and views of themselves, alongside a positive attitude to learning. We have much to learn from our counterparts in Europe on how we teach children listening and memory skills, the ability to be attentive and the behaviour acceptable in group situations. Through drama, adults have the possibility of strongly promoting social skills and cooperation. Drama is also valuable in the development of self-management, reflection, attention, persistence and other personal skills.

Curriculum Guidance for the Foundation Stage (DfEE/QCA 2000b: 32) gives pointers for practitioners as to how the goals might be achieved. In this area of learning, the document states that 'Practitioners who understand the importance of role play in children's personal, social and emotional development' are needed for effective teaching. It illustrates this point with the following statement:

> Children learn many skills and attitudes in well-planned role play. It encourages individual and cooperative play and gives children opportunities to express feelings, to use language, to develop literacy and numeracy skills and to learn without failure. Role play gives children the opportunity to make sense of their world. It is sometimes useful to have two scenarios such as the home and the shop, which allows children to make connections in their learning.

Welcome as any mention of the importance of role play is, this statement again highlights the lack of knowledge, even by practitioners, of the complexity of the use of the pretend self. The statement encourages good practice in socio-dramatic play but does not support the effectiveness of thematic-fantasy play or the importance of adult intervention in the creation of narrative.

Piaget's seminal work on pretence in the early 1950s (Piaget 1952) provided a widely accepted theory that emphasized the symbolic nature of pretend – e.g. a child's ability to use one object to represent another (a piece of cloth that represents a pillow). His theory was based on observations of solitary and parallel play, typically the kind of play exhibited in socio-dramatic settings.

We would like to suggest that the social interaction required in group dramatic activity, in either the home or educational setting, goes beyond an individual child's ability to make symbolic relationships for themselves. It encourages children to develop their ability to make sense of another's assumed use of imaginary objects and events. Research has shown (Harris and Kavanaugh 1993) that 2-year-old children are able to respond to a researcher's imagined play where both real and imagined objects are used. The children tested revealed that they not only understood the 'make-believe' created by another (in this instance an adult) but also that they were able to respond to it appropriately. This leads us to believe in the importance of pretend play as a medium for learning in personal and social development.

Organization of personal, social and emotional development learning goals

Early Learning Goals (DfEE/QCA 1999a) gives 14 goals relating to personal, social and emotional development. By placing these under four broad headings we have a more manageable organization for assessment. Working alongside our children in drama, the broad headings give us a very effective tool to observe all the aspects of the required objectives (see Table 4.1).

Behaviour to learn

As children engage in drama with their existing knowledge we the practitioners aim to facilitate some new learning. Through drama we are helping children to understand the world around them, a world that is rapidly changing. We aim to develop the skills, attitudes and knowledge needed not only to meet the challenges they will face both daily and in the future but also to enable them to become lifelong learners.

To stay motivated to learn, children need to be given exciting and interesting activities that maintain their attention. It has been our experience that when children are exploring new ideas in drama they are given the most powerful 'need to know'. For example, a group of 6-year-olds, needing to travel from one island to another, decided that the giant beetles on one island could fly. They agreed that this would be their means of transport and that they would undertake the journey at the beginning of the next session. During the following week, several boys raided the school

Table 4.1 The 14 goals for personal, social and emotional development under four broad headings

Behaviour to learn	Social integration	Consequences of behaviour	Personal identity and responsibility
• Continue to be interested, excited and motivated to learn; • be confident to try new activities, initiate ideas and speak in a familiar group; • maintain attention, concentrate, and sit quietly when appropriate.	• Have a developing awareness of their own needs, views and feelings and be sensitive to the needs, views and feelings of others; • have a developing respect for their own cultures and beliefs and those of other people; • form good relationships with adults and peers; • work as part of a group or class, taking turns and sharing fairly, understanding that there need to be agreed values and codes of behaviour for groups of people, including adults and children, to work together harmoniously.	• Understand what is right and wrong and why; • consider the consequences of their words and actions for themselves and others; • understand people have different needs, views, cultures and beliefs, which need to be treated with respect.	• Respond to significant experiences, showing a range of feelings when appropriate; • dress and undress independently and manage their own personal hygiene; • select and use activities and resources independently; • understand that they can expect others to treat their needs, views, cultures and beliefs with respect.

Source: Adapted from DfEE/QCA (1999a) *Early Learning Goals.*

library in search of books on insects. They drew and wrote about five beetles they discovered could fly and presented their findings to the other children at the opening of the next session. There was growing interest from the group as to which beetle to choose before the story could be resumed. This group of children had their attention held by their friends and sat quietly without interrupting, listening attentively.

Children who find out facts and details because they need to know them for a story often carry this information with them for a very long time. On a recent visit to a primary school, an 11-year-old girl greeted the drama practitioner in the corridor. 'Do you remember me?' she said. 'I was in the story about the frogs and a toad when I was in reception.' She proceeded to tell the story she and her friends had created and gave quite detailed descriptions of the life cycle of frogs and toads that had been necessary for the story. If you give children factual information during a drama it is important that it is correct!

By using drama as the forum for learning, children are confident to try new activities and initiate ideas. David (1999: 2) reminds us that 'the first eight years of life cover an important period of change and development in children's thinking and in their ability to make sense of the world'. Imaginative approaches to teaching in the early years are at the heart of producing creative learners for life.

Social integration

There is an overwhelming need to see personal, social and emotional development not as a separate 'subject' area but as an integral part of all aspects of teaching and learning in the early years. Being a social activity, drama requires children to develop and use their social skills to engage in it. As it is an interactive, *social* art form, shaped by the social context in which it is created, drama becomes the ideal vehicle for exploring the social progress of children. It is not an activity that is easily undertaken on your own; it is more satisfactory as a shared experience. Wherever the drama takes place – in the home, preschool or school setting – the principles and beliefs of the group involved and the individual knowledge, attitudes, values and experiences of the participants will influence the outcome. The social context, ethos or culture of a group is particularly relevant to drama.

Drama is shaped and influenced by social context and as such relies heavily on the positive social interaction of its participants. When taking part in drama we are asking children, with commitment and integrity, to adopt a pretend self and engage in a fictional context. This requires trust between participants as well as between participants and the facilitator. In some situations trust may be established quickly and with ease, but when it is absent, and due to the need to develop basic social skills, then building trust becomes a priority.

Drama is reliant on social skills and can develop such skills if appropriate and carefully structured experiences are offered. If a group of children appears to be unable to work together, then there is all the more reason for offering them drama. No children, however poor their social skills, should be denied dramatic play. We simply have to start from where the children are. This may mean that for some time personal development takes priority. Children may need drama experiences that primarily promote listening skills or turn taking, or a foundation of small group work (maybe in the role play area, for example), before embarking on a larger group drama session.

Dealing with challenging behaviour

Adopting another self offers safety and protection from which to develop an awareness of needs, views and feelings. Children are protected by the fact that they are undertaking an adopted role. Children who display difficult or challenging behaviour sometimes continue to do so because it has become expected of them. In drama they can behave in a new way, free from predicted expectations. By taking on the alternative role, the child can be released from anticipated behaviours and placed in a position where there is the opportunity to behave in an uncharacteristic manner. Often children who have reputations for antisocial behaviour and unkindness to others will perform with insight and sensitivity within the protection of a story. Adults can use an adopted role (teacher in role) to confront or challenge difficulties.

Adults working with a group of 4-year-olds from a challenging environment found that, using interactive story-making, they were able to help these children work as part of a group, take turns and agree on codes of behaviour. The group topic was 'castles' and the children were in role as servants to the king and queen. The adults adopted a lower status role as new servants who needed training. This placed the children in the 'mantle of the expert.' The first 10 to 15 minutes were chaotic. Children ran around the drama space and would not accept their role as trainers. Instead of stopping the session the adults persevered and were rewarded for their trust:

David: Fire! Fire! [He runs to an adult helper and looks at her.] Fire! Fire!! [He points to the corner of the space.]

Adult: Where's the fire coming from?

David: Down there!
[The other children become interested and gather around the adults.]

Ben: It's the dungeon.

Adult: Is there anyone in the dungeon?

Ben: A dragon.

Adult: Oh my! I don't think I've ever seen a dragon!

Sophie: They can breathe fire.

Adult: Can they? Do you think it's the dragon making the fire then?

Ben: He's locked up.
           [The adults sit the children in a group on the floor to discuss the dilemma. In the course of the discussion Maria runs to the corner and comes back.]

Maria: The dragon has told me she has babies and she wants to take them home.

Adult: Where does the dragon live?

Maria: I'll go and ask her.
           [She leaves the group again. The children remain silent as they listen to Maria talking to the dragon. She returns.]

Maria: On an island a long way from here.

Adult: Gosh! How on earth will we get her there?

Ben: Wise Owl will know.

Adult: Wise Owl?

Ben: He lives in the wood.

Maria: The dragon's calling, I can hear her.
           [Everyone gets up to follow. There is some noise. Maria puts her finger to her lips and all become silent. They tip-toe to speak to the dragon.]

Maria: She says Wise Owl will know.

The story continued for a further 50 minutes and had to conclude because it was hometime. This example shows how children, when they are engrossed in the story-making discipline, find a huge capacity for concentration. Of course, not all the children were engaged all the time, but unlike other situations those who chose to take 'time out' did not try to disrupt what was happening. An implicit code of behaviour had been established by the children that they did not wish to challenge.

Providing a positive culture

Whatever the objective, drama and social development are inextricably linked and skills in each will develop simultaneously. When children have regular opportunities to engage in dramatic activity, either at home or in another setting, they will develop their skills of sharing, listening and cooperating. They will learn about working as a member of a group, valuing contributions made by others and developing empathy through participating or observing others in role. It is essential that children are able to respect others and respect differences in culture and belief. We are not implying that children should have acquired these skills before experiencing drama, but that drama will serve to develop them.

As children extend their play, they move from the socio-dramatic mode of 'acting out' familiar scenarios to the introduction of dilemmas. These might include Dad leaving home, Mum giving birth or someone dying. The children introduce elements from their own differing home lives that they wish to explore through the pretend play. Each child brings to the pretend situation an internalized history of personal and social experience, based on situations lived out in the past.

To be able to form good relationships with adults and peers, children need to know that what they are going to be made to do will not make them feel uncomfortable. To work as part of a group requires a strong sense of trust. Many adults who recoil at the thought of drama (because it revives nightmare images of their so-called drama experiences at school) probably had their trust in adults broken. Being put on the spot and asked to improvise, or told to read the part of a character from a play aloud in front of the class is more likely to hinder personal and social growth than extend it.

We have already discussed the difference between taking on a role and performing. The adoption of a pretend self is central to drama and when adopting the pretend self children have the opportunity to step into the shoes of, and behave as if they are, someone other than themselves. Some children may find it difficult to trust the ambivalence of this process, but generally children adapt with ease, as this is something they instinctively do in their play. They can be helped through the drama to forge positive interactions and relationships with their peers. Working 'harmoniously' together is not a problem when all the participants understand the 'game' and agree on the codes and values of the group.

Role reversal

As we have already seen (see p. 57), role reversal is used to encourage children to function in different ways. The children, rather than the adult, are placed in high-status roles that offer the opportunity to make decisions and control situations. The very quiet, shy child can become a leader or hero, protecting the other children from a monster. The child who struggles academically can become an expert on flying, guiding the class on a journey to the moon. In such instances children are empowered – they learn to respect and value themselves. Their peers, who often see them anew, learn to respect them too. Through adopting a role children can be given a voice and a forum where their ideas will be valued and interaction with their peers developed. They might have to care, or be cared for, protect or be protected, share, take turns, make decisions.

Although this takes place within the drama, the children then have a common experience through which they are united and have developed skills in citizenship to carry forward into real-life situations. They have had the opportunity to experience this in a safe, secure environment.

Consequences of behaviour

Experiencing and controlling a social situation through drama is not only empowering, but also very enlightening. Children begin to understand why people behave in certain ways when placed in certain situations, because they are scared, angry, jealous, sad and so on. They are able to explore what makes them feel angry, scared or sad and to see how they feel and respond when placed in different situations. As they interact with others, they find out how their ideas about life, morals and behaviour compare with those of others.

For example, some 3-year-old children who were involved in a story taking place on the moon met a moon monster. Two little girls previously not known for their care of others in normal play situations were, along with the other children, hostile to the monster, played by an adult:

Jessica: Go away, we hate you!
           [Other children begin to hiss and scream at the 'monster'.]
Monster   [begins to cry]: Why are you being nasty to me? I don't want to hurt. I can't help being a monster.
           [As the adult in role as monster began to draw attention to her feelings and reacted to the ill-will by pretending to cry, the two little girls came forward to comfort her.]
Jessica: I'll look after you.
Monster: Oh! Thank you. You are very kind. I feel better now.
Debra   [to the children]: Sh! You're upsetting him.
           [They began to reprimand the other children for their unkindness.]

To confirm their contribution, the 'monster' and the other adult roles in the story praised the girls' actions. They really had saved the monster, but at the same time had been given some insight into the feelings of others.

Parents at home can distract a child who is having a temper tantrum, for instance, by pretending that a favourite soft toy is upset by the all noise: 'Big Bear doesn't like all the noise. He's crying. Can you help me comfort him?' Through this use of 'pretend' the child can be encouraged to 'comfort' the toy and at the same time perhaps gain some understanding of the consequences of their own behaviour.

The importance of moral development

In our world of change, opportunity and choice, there is a growing concern about morality, and the ability of young people to make moral decisions. By taking as our meaning of morality the theory of Kohlberg that 'morality represents a set of rational principles of judgement and decisions valid for every culture, the principles of welfare and justice' (Winston 1998: 13), we have a wider understanding that takes us beyond the call for 'traditional values' or 'back to basics'.

Curriculum 2000 (DfEE/QCA 1999b) highlights the importance of children having opportunities to explore moral issues and the responsibility of teachers to challenge prejudice and stereotypical assumptions. The curriculum also includes a statement of commonly consented values regarding the self, relationships, society and the environment. It is important that such issues are addressed. Living in a richly diverse society that is working towards equality of opportunity for all, it is important that children have some experience of what this means.

Returning to the 'ideational potential' of drama, children's existing perceptions can be explored by working through dilemma – particularly moral dilemma. The quandary is a strong characteristic of drama work and although you do not always have to pose a complication, more often than not children will create one if it is absent. It is the dilemma that engages and focuses the interest. It gives a purpose and places children in the position of problem setters, problem solvers and decision makers. Children gain great satisfaction from dealing with complex issues that are usually the domain of adults. Through drama we are creating situations, rich with dilemma, in order to offer children opportunities to make decisions, see the implications of those decisions and pose alternatives.

For example, during one interactive story, the adult and children were mice who came under threat from an imagined cat. One of the boys in the class produced a gun and wanted to shoot the cat in order to protect the others. The adult could have simply told this particular boy that she did not like guns and did not want any in the story. Instead, in role as a mouse with the class, she gathered them together and faced them with the dilemma. The children eventually decided that the owners of the cat would be terribly upset if the mice shot it and set about suggesting other ways of solving the problem and protecting themselves. In role, the adult had helped the children solve the problem of the gun from within the context, by generating the children's ideas and opinions.

The children addressed the dilemma with passion and thought because it was in a real context and they were going to have to face the implications. The boy with the gun had the opportunity to view the situation from various angles and was made aware of alternative possibilities. The learning and negotiation that had taken place would never have been so considered or so important to the children if the adult had just decided to discuss guns in a circle-time one day. The drama created a real dilemma, requiring a solution within the context of the story.

The 'authentic voice'

There will be times when children reveal or disclose worrying, sensitive or inappropriate ideas or information. This often presents itself when children introduce issues that are significant to themselves and are part of their own real world. They may suggest violent methods of punishment or indicate fears about the dark which are more than creative suggestions. We call this 'the authentic voice' as it is the voice of the real child heard in the imaginary situation. It is important that we do not simply dismiss or reprimand their offerings, but find an appropriate way of catering for them. Such disclosures should be treated in the same way as any other 'children at risk' information is used.

Creating a safe environment with trust and respect is not only the responsibility of adults, but of the children as well. If we aim to empower children through the use of drama then part of this is children taking responsibility for their emotions and their behaviour and being able to define what they think is appropriate or inappropriate, and why.

In order to achieve this we have to 'slow down' or pause the action to allow exploration and consideration of the situation. This is where the use of reflection becomes significant. By 'freezing' the action, we allow children the opportunity to reflect in role or out of role. This helps the children to focus on how they feel in certain situations or to empathize with others. They begin to consider actions and consequences, understand and respect differing points of view and develop new perspectives.

Focusing on significant moments

By replaying significant moments several times, we can revisit a situation or event and each time witness how different behaviour produces different outcomes. This technique is more appropriate for 5- and 6-year-olds when they are beginning to have a clearer understanding of cause and effect. Through drama, children discover how feelings, behaviour and attitudes are influenced by different circumstances, conflicts and pressures. This becomes a group understanding and might change the functioning of the group but not necessarily individual children within it.

Personal identity and responsibility

Winnicott (1971) suggested that certain conditions had to be present if a child was successfully going to find themselves as a person. His most essential element in this process was creativity. The child, when engaged in play – and only play – is able to be fully creative which leads eventually to a point where 'the individual discovers the self'.

We make full use of the natural ability to be creative by engaging in drama and by employing adult intervention to add structure and form to the process. Previous chapters have indicated that sensitive and informed intervention by an adult maximizes the learning potential of play and offers children an opportunity to learn by engaging in a medium with which they are familiar and in which they have expertise. As adults we structure the drama to offer experiences relevant to the needs of each particular group of children. This may be the opportunity to explore a familiar situation or event, or the chance to apply knowledge and understanding to a new situation. Both socio-dramatic and thematic-fantasy play are highly social methods of learning and have a positive effect on personal, social and emotional development.

It is most important to clarify that we are not asking children to act or perform. The drama may incorporate theatrical aspects, or the children may instinctively employ elements of theatre form. For example, they may create tension, use silence or use objects symbolically. When we are using drama as a process for learning, our primary concern is not to develop theatrical or performance skills. We are looking at drama as a process that exists for the present experience, not something to be repeated for performance. We would therefore not encourage elaborate characterization, or costumes, but would require integrity to the adopted role.

We are asking children to behave 'as if' they are someone other than themselves. They are not acting but being. Performance, as we explain later, requires other kinds of skills. What is important for personal and social development is an element of detachment that allows us to look outside the role, reflect and learn from the situation. A vital aspect of the drama process is that it is interactive and operates through negotiation with others. Therefore, the responsibility for the drama becomes a shared responsibility.

Building self-esteem
Real life moves too fast. To see something more clearly we need to step aside and distance ourselves from a situation. Children who feel low self-worth need experiences where they can feel good about themselves. In drama, by playing with time and place, we create opportunities for such children to be given positive reinforcement. The action of the drama can be stopped at significant moments, by freezing an instant in time, to explore characters' feelings and intentions, or to discuss choices and outcomes. This helps children to develop their growing sense of identity, as they learn about themselves and others through the safety of an imagined context. They learn about their strengths, their character, their likes and dislikes.

Feelings can be experienced and examined through the safety and

protection of the pretend self. By using role play areas, engaging in interactive storytelling or using drama conventions, children can experiment
with a variety of different selves and behaviours. Perspectives and
responsibilities that are usually the property of adults can be experienced
in the imaginary context. What has been learned from these imagined
experiences children can later transfer to the real life situations they
encounter.

Children are offered the opportunity momentarily to step outside the
action and reflect; being both participants and spectators at one and the
same time. Participating in the creation of the drama and commenting on
its content and direction give children a powerful learning tool. This ability to reflect is not only important for drama, but as a life skill.

The development of personal and emotional skills

The unique nature of drama is that it operates on two levels. On one level
the child, with his or her own knowledge and experiences, is operating
within the social context of the preschool, nursery or school setting. On
another level they are asked to engage in imaginary contexts and adopt
imaginary selves. Holding these two worlds in their head at the same time
allows, as has already been discussed, a duality of action to take place.

Application of knowledge and understanding from the real world to the
imaginary, where it is confirmed or refined and transferred, can be used
again in the real world. The children are, if you like, rehearsing for life.
Adults often employ this strategy. Before an important event such as an
interview, we may role play that situation in order to learn how we can
manipulate it successfully. We will then apply this learning to the real-life
situation. This is a significant feature of drama. It is not designed to intimi-
date people or put them on the spot but to offer a safe environment to learn
about, and rehearse for, life.

The development of the emotions

Goleman (1996: 4) suggests that:

> the very name *Homo sapiens*, the thinking species, is misleading in the
> light of the new appreciation and vision of the place of emotions in
> our lives that science now offers. As we all know from experience,
> when it comes to shaping our decisions and our actions, feeling
> counts every bit as much – and often more – than thought.

We have two processes that drive our thinking: our rational self and our
emotional self. Our impulse to act is often driven by our emotional not our
rational self. In most situations, both sides feed each other, with the

emotional and the rational in harmony. But as a nation we have problems with an excess of emotion in times of stress: 'boys don't cry' for example. The term 'stiff upper lip' comes from a fear of raw emotion where it is seen as the loss of control.

The emotional response of very young children to a situation will often take precedence over any rational reasoning. It is our job, as educators, to help children not to repress their emotional self but to understand and work with it for the sake of their later lives. Goleman (1996) tells of an experiment called the 'marshmallow challenge' in which preschool children were told they could have two marshmallows if they could wait beside the marshmallows until the researcher returned. Some children were able to wait by using distracting tactics such as singing, covering their eyes or playing games. Others grabbed the marshmallows as soon as the researcher left. What is remarkable about this research was the follow up some 14 years later. It was found that those children who at 4 were able to resist temptation were now 'more socially competent: personally effective, self-assertive, and better able to cope with the frustrations of life' (1996: 81). However, the other young people were more likely to retreat from social contacts, be indecisive and intractable and were easily upset by frustrations.

Understanding emotions and the minds of other people is essential if children are to relate to other people. Dunn (1988) found that children who had engaged in 'pretend play' with their siblings as 2-year-olds were particularly successful at understanding other minds in formal assessments. They were more likely to take account of a rival's viewpoint and to communicate in a connected manner with others.

Non-verbal language

As there is an aural language from which children make meaning there is also a visual language. Dramatic activity deals with both the verbal and the non-verbal and it is a very useful tool to observe the play of 1–2-year-olds. Through these observations we have a potent medium to explore the emotional self. By playing and replaying a situation, children use the 'pretend' to explore feelings of happiness, excitement, uncertainty, anger, fear, sadness, grief, suffering and so on. By watching them play, adults can attempt to gauge how they might be feeling and thinking.

Drama provides us with a form and structure for investigating significant issues that arise, and also gives a distance to the issues, affording protection. When a child has experienced a death in the family, for example, parents and early years workers could explore the theme of loss through a story about the loss of a teddy bear. Using this method, we are finding a parallel situation where the context is changed and distanced, but some of the feelings encountered remain the same. Within the security of the drama, children can investigate ways of dealing with loss and ways of supporting others who have suffered loss. In the 'moon monster' example given earlier (see p. 60) an adult in role was able to express and display feelings of hurt and upset in a way that made showing emotions acceptable and helpful.

Preschool children may not be ready to reflect out of role on the situation but they are capable of responding to it. They can read the non-verbal elements of a person's emotional reaction. By the age of 2, children are beginning not only to recognize emotions in others but to talk about their own feelings. Research has shown that if mothers draw attention to unkind behaviour and its effect on others, children are more likely to show concern and kindness as a result (Dunn 1988). It is important therefore that discussion should immediately follow an incident of this sort. The power to change understanding is reduced in proportion to the time which elapses between an event and talking about it.

Reflecting on emotions

Reflection may also take place at the end of a session and as such it provides an opportunity to discuss various issues raised in the drama, or how dilemmas were solved. At the same time, parallels can be made between the difficulties in the story and the children's own lives.

Although the drama may have been about 'Jack and the Beanstalk', there would have been many layers of meaning relevant to the children's own lives. For example, Jack swaps his cow for beans from an old man he meets on the way to market, because he trusts that the beans are magic. He believes he has done the right thing, but his mother is furious. To draw parallels from this situation, you might ask the children if they have ever been in trouble for doing something they thought was right and how it felt. Have they ever done anything thinking they were being helpful, but got into trouble? Have they ever trusted someone and been let down? The context of the drama becomes less important and the inner experience more so.

Through reflection, children are offered the opportunity to identify with a wider range of human issues and to consider the relevance of those issues to their lives. It can be a way of accessing and understanding difficult or remote situations. The children may feel that they have little in common with the character they have been playing, but the feelings involved are something that both have experienced. Suddenly something very remote has personal significance, and a new understanding has developed.

Adult observation and intervention

Adult observation is a critical part of the intervention and reflection process. Throughout the drama session the role of the adult is delicately balanced, particularly in relation to their stance regarding any dilemmas or issues raised. If the adult remains neutral there is the danger that a variety of views or the complexity of issues will not be realized. The adult may fail to intervene and develop and deepen the potential level of understanding. On the other hand, by demonstrating commitment to an issue, the adult may deter other opinions. By teaching didactically, we are saying that this is 'not an issue', because there is only this one interpretation of it (Bolton: 1984).

Adults in role

Adults may choose to take on role for a variety of reasons. By stepping into the shoes of, and behaving as if they were, someone other than themselves, they can focus the children's attention on the need to question a character or make a group decision so that the drama can proceed. The aim of adopting role may be to give information, to pose an alternative viewpoint, or to help the group come to a collective agreement.

It is important to think about the status of the role that is adopted and how this influences the status of the children. If you, the adult, are in a low-status role, such as a frightened, lost bear, the children are placed automatically in a high-status role where they are in control of caring for you. The real-life status of both children and teacher are reversed and the children are empowered. Just as role provides protection for the children, so it does for adults.

Educational drama and drama therapy

Through educational drama we offer the children the opportunity to replay life or engage in new experiences through a fictional context. This allows us to examine with them how their behaviour and interactions affect different situations. However, we must be careful not to misuse our role as adults in this process. Although educational drama allows us to examine behaviour and how it affects others it is not our role to alter behaviour in a therapy sense. We are not in the business of 'modifying' behaviour and must be conscientious not to stray into the world of 'drama therapy'. The play/drama therapist works with different and specialized goals that should not be attempted by an untrained person.

Jennings (1999: 51), a drama therapist, states the 'reskilling and empowerment' of children as one of her primary aims. She goes on to say, 'In dramatic playing children find resolutions, change reality, invent worlds and develop their imagination usually within the protected world of grown-ups'. In this kind of environment the adult workers know a great deal about each child. The play situations are carefully chosen and take place with one child or a very small group of children who are very closely monitored. Such work takes time and often sessions will last much longer than an allotted period in an educational setting. We must remember that in education sometimes up to 30 or more children are taking part in a group story-making session.

Conclusion

Through using dramatic activity, we constantly learn about the children in our care as they expose their immense potential, experiences and knowledge of the world. As we learn about children, as individuals and members of a group, we can devise drama experiences that meet their needs. A child's achievement in drama is not dependent on academic ability, gender, confidence or culture, but on the way in which all these qualities combine to enable children to create meaning with others. For children to become socially competent and personally effective adults they need to have a strong sense of self. To enable them to develop fulfilled adult lives we feel that children need opportunities to:

- manage uncertainty and change;
- develop identity and a sense of self;
- develop morality and the ability to make moral decisions;
- work cooperatively with others;
- foster a playful disposition.

Summary

This chapter has identified that:

- children learn many skills and attitudes in well-planned role play;
- drama gives children the opportunity to make sense of their world and the worlds of others;
- as children engage in drama with their existing knowledge, we the practitioners facilitate new learning;
- being a social activity, drama requires children to develop and use their social skills to engage in it;
- if children have poor social skills, then there is all the more reason for offering them drama;
- real emotions and feelings can be shared and expressed;

- through drama, children's ideas are genuinely listened to, valued and acted upon, by both adults and other children;
- the real-life status of both children and teacher are reversed and the children are empowered;
- the drama form creates real dilemmas;
- educational drama should not be confused with drama therapy.

5

Drama and the whole child

Education influences and reflects the values of society, and the
kind of society we want to be. It is important therefore to
recognise a broad set of common values and purposes that
underpin the school curriculum and the work of schools.

(DfEE/QCA 1999b: 10)

'The whole curriculum', for most practitioners, suggests the delivery of
the main headings of *Early Learning Goals* (DfEE/QCA 1999a) such as
language, mathematics, knowledge and understanding of the world.
Although *Early Learning Goals* maintains the subject-based curriculum
there are signs at last that the early years foundation stage is being recognized as a discrete phase of education. For the first time there is acknow-
ledgement that play is an important learning tool.

Curriculum 2000, like its predecessor, strongly supports a subject-based
curriculum but it now also includes an element of key skills. These are
described as 'six skill areas . . . [to] help learners improve their learning
and performance in education, work and life' (DfEE/QCA 1999b). These
skills include communication, application of number, information technology, working with others, improving own learning and performance,
problem solving and thinking skills. Along with these, practitioners are
asked to consider citizenship, gender, special needs and multicultural
issues.

In this chapter, we look at the role of drama in the new curriculum and
examine how drama can support the wider needs of the whole child.
As drama practitioners, our aim is to make a significant contribution towards the development of the whole child. This needs to go beyond their
knowledge and understanding of a prescribed curriculum to encom-
pass knowledge about themselves and others and the world in which
they live.

Experts in play and drama

We would like to advance a reason for the exclusion of drama as a named subject from the revision of the early years curriculum. If you examine the literature, there has been very little crossover between early years practitioners writing about early years pretend play and those writing about 'process drama'. There is without doubt a dearth of articles and books written by drama practitioners solely for those working with preschool and early years children. There are papers and texts by psychologists and play experts on the importance and effects of pretend play on the curriculum (Kitson 1994; Smith 1994; Beardsley 1998) but very little has been produced specifically for early years settings that explains how drama could be used in a developmental curriculum.

Drama practitioners and play experts have much in common and a considerable amount to learn from each other about the developmental curriculum. A great deal has been written and campaigned for in recent years about an appropriate curriculum for the early years. There is agreement among early years practitioners, which includes the editors and contributors to this series, that a developmentally appropriate curriculum is extremely important. All the principles set out in the preface of this book could apply to the principles of teaching drama in the early years: 'The role of the educator of young children is to engage actively with what concerns the child, and to support learning through these occupations' (Hurst and Joseph 1998) could be the axiom for this text.

The importance of a thematic approach in drama planning

Cross-curricular themes that were the main strategy for teaching nursery, reception and beyond before the advent of the National Curriculum, although deficient in some respects, did provide a continuity and cohesion for young children. They often contained the notion of a 'developmentally appropriate' curriculum. With the publication of *Desirable Outcomes* (DfEE/SCAA 1996) some curricular planning began to put subject requirements before the needs of individual children. In the many settings that have maintained thematic work, subtle changes have been brought about to the former approach by adopting a form of planning that visibly separates the theme into subject divisions. This can result in a failure to address the needs and developmental learning demands of young children.

Early years children do not perceive the world segmented into different subject areas. Neither do they view their environment in the objective manner required of subject-focused activity. Such approaches to the curriculum create a fragmentation of thinking that is not recognizable to the very young mind.

In recent directives, whole class teaching is encouraged and seen as the important feature of the new provision. In the *Annual Report of Her Majesty's Inspector of Schools* (Ofsted 2000), Chris Woodhead observed that 'Whole-class teaching is both common and more skilful than it once was'. Interestingly, drama has always been a whole-class activity but with the needs of the individual, not a subject area, at its heart. As Neelands (1992: 39) observes, 'If curriculum planning begins with establishing how the child will view the theme *before* it goes on to map out the learning potential through reference to attainment targets or discrete areas of educational experience, then the problems of fragmentation and sequencing learning effectively pale'.

A *curriculum of two dimensions*

'Curriculum 2000' (DfEE/QCA 1999b) has in part acknowledged this through its proposal for the curriculum to have two dimensions. The first dimension is that of providing 'opportunities for all pupils to learn and to achieve'. The second is 'to promote spiritual, moral, social, and cultural development and prepare all pupils for the opportunities, responsibilities and experiences of life'. In preparing children for 'life' this leads us to ask the question, what will life in the future be like for the young children of today? What skills, attitudes, knowledge, experiences, qualities, morals, will children need in order to succeed in this life?

The world of the future

It is impossible to project into the future and predict how life will change. Seventeen to twenty years from now, when the children with whom we currently work will be adults, life will be very different. Exactly how society, families, relationships, morality and the working world will alter, we do not know but it is safe to assume they will.

Current trends in the workplace seem to suggest that there will be more jobs involving intellectual work and computers rather than manual work. With an increase in unemployment, a global economy and job insecurity, it would be safe to assume that the future is uncertain and that employment will have a more transient nature. A changing working world requires people with different kinds of skills, knowledge and resources. It demands the ability to live with uncertainty, to be adaptable and not deterred by rejection. But we must also prepare our children for a life beyond work. How do we want them to use their leisure time and their retirement, which for many could be longer than their working lives?

Social and moral life is also changing; people have more opportunities and choice about what they will do and think. Roles are less prescribed and confined and many aspects of life are less traditional. People now have more freedom to be individual and choose their direction, rather than have it prescribed by their family, culture, class or religion. Despite all the positive aspects of a changing society, it can leave people unsure of their identity, their role in life, and with an uncertainty about expectations. There is speculation that in the not too distant future the ethnic white population of Great Britain will be outnumbered by the population who have their origins in other faiths and cultures.

Increased freedom in terms of how you are going to live your life brings with it a greater responsibility in terms of making choices. As Guy Claxton, a professor of psychology stated at an early education conference in 1999, 'We've become a generation of choosers rather than receivers'. We therefore have to help children to become good decision makers and moral decision makers, able to cope with choice, freedom and uncertainty. Developing an appropriate curriculum for a world we cannot perceive is a challenging task.

Promoting effective thinking

One thing is certain, children who acquire effective thinking skills will be at a strong advantage over their counterparts. A 'thinking skills' curriculum is a new but exciting concept in British education that has already been an influence on curriculum development in the USA and elsewhere. There is now a strong movement to improve the teaching of thinking (Fisher 1990; Costello 2000), but as drama practitioners we would argue that drama has always had the skills of thinking, especially reasoning and argument, at its core.

You cannot engage young children in the problems confronting the huntsman in 'Snow White' or the dilemma faced by King Midas without involving them in the process of thinking and reasoning. Following some work on Judith Nicholls' (1985) poem 'Midas', some 5- and 6-year-olds were put in the role of servants employed by Midas. After a session of 'hot seating' where an adult in role as Midas had been interviewed by the children, the children decided to move into the 'living picture' of Midas entering the cave of Lord Bacchus to receive his gift. Before he could make his entry, Daniel, aged 6, got down on one knee and begged his master to rethink his desire for the golden touch. He very lucidly argued his case by pointing out the harm and upset it may cause to all the people King Midas would meet: 'Please don't do this. It will make everyone miserable. You will change everything into gold. All your servants [he indicates the other children] will be changed into gold. Your food will turn to gold. You could turn to gold. We want you to think very carefully about what you are about to do.'

Through dramatic activity, we can encourage our children to become critical thinkers. To do this we must ourselves think beyond subject-based objectives that promote factual learning and ask what thinking skills people will need in the twenty-first century. Most situations we encounter in life require us to draw on knowledge from several subject areas. We need to be able to synthesize what we know to formulate any credible answers. By engaging children in situations that require them to use their knowledge and understanding to both set and solve problems and make decisions, we help them to have ownership of their own knowledge.

Sparks-Linfield and Warwick (1996: 94) describe how a teacher colleague used drama to assess science and her children's understanding of magnets. The results were surprising. The children who had been able to complete the tests for magnets in the classroom had in fact a limited understanding of the property of metals. On the other hand, those who had found the class tests uninteresting performed at a much higher level of understanding when they were asked to use their knowledge in a drama situation.

The comments of the teacher, having used this method of assessment, were revealing. She said:

> Although I've often carried out assessments of science I've always done them as part of classroom activities. The story and drama has put the science in the real world. It has shown me who understands, who doesn't know what metal is and who needs to have a lot more practical experience of magnets.
>
> (Sparks-Linfield and Warwick 1996: 94)

Children sometimes do not know what they know until they are asked to talk about it. For example, a 5-year-old was taking part in a story about farms. The tanker taking the milk to market broke down and another was called. The second tanker was smaller than the first. The children discussed their knowledge of 'siphoning' and began to move the milk from one tanker to another. James became very agitated and called for everyone to stop. He told us that the milk from the big tanker would spill over in a minute because the little tanker 'did not have enough space inside for all the milk'. James did not need to demonstrate through any tests that he knew about capacity – his understanding was plain to see.

Through adopting roles, children have to think and speak in a variety of contexts, often outside their everyday experience. They may be involved in a debate, an argument, in persuasion or in comforting. In the following example, working with 4-year-old children, we brought to life the story 'The Toy's Party' from the Oxford Reading Tree Scheme to explore the unspoken scenes. The young boy Kipper makes a terrible mess in the kitchen trying to create a birthday cake for his toys. When his mother finally sees the mess in the kitchen the only text we are offered is 'Mum was angry'. The children created the dialogue that was missing from the story. What did Mum say? What did Kipper say? The children, in turn, adopted the role of Mum. We extended the story by providing the conversation that took place when Mum found the terrible mess that Kipper had made. The adult, seated in a chair, took the role of Kipper. The children, in role as Mum, left the circle and made an entrance to signify the beginning of their role:

Karen [using an angry voice]: Look at the mess you have made!

Adult: I was making a cake.

Karen: You mustn't do that without Mummy . . . You used all the beans. We were going to have those for tea.

Adult: But I wanted a party and a cake.

Karen: Not without Mummy and Daddy. We were only outside . . . er . . . washing the car. [Karen is using her knowledge of the text here. She remembers Kipper's thought bubble showing Mum and Dad washing the car together.]

Adult: Sorry.

Karen: You have to go, you go to your room now. We've got to put your clothes on the washing line. [Here again she uses her knowledge of the text. The final picture in the book shows Mum hanging Kipper's clothes on the line.]
[Zara takes Karen's place as Mum.]

Zara [shouting extremely loudly]: Kipper! [There is a long pause. Adult in role as Kipper is shocked by the shouting.] Look at the mess you have made.

Adult: I was making a cake.

Zara: You've used all the jam, we were going to have that for tea. [Here Zara is using Karen's idea, but substitutes the beans with the jam.]

Adult [offering the spoon]: Do you want to taste it?

Zara: No. Take your clothes off, we'll have to wash them.

Drama can be used to speak the silences of stories, or to change the direction of stories, or to create alternative endings. Working in this way, along with energetic discussion and reflection, children use language in exciting contexts and in the process we can meet many of the required speaking and listening objectives of the National Curriculum (Speaking and Listening at Key Stage 1).

During another session, using an interactive story, we were building an imaginary rocket. The location of the story was in a house and the children spoke in detail about the kinds of equipment they would need to build the rocket. They gave reasons for the suitability of the materials they chose, such as its strength, and discussed various joining techniques. They thought through each phase of making the rocket very carefully. Although it was not intentionally planned, this became an excellent piece of design technology.

Having built our imaginary rocket that was to take us to the moon, we painted it. We then decided that we needed to get into the rocket and prepare for take off. The belief and understanding of the context was strong. As we were climbing into the rocket one of the children reminded everyone that the paint was still wet, in case it got on anybody's clothes. At this point, one of the boys created the first complication. We had constructed the rocket inside the house and there was no way we could launch it. The rocket, he also informed us, was far too big to fit through the doors of the house. Although the rocket was imaginary, this child had a very strong image in his head. In terms of numeracy objectives, he was working in a meaningful and practical context, problem solving, communicating, using mathematical language and immersing other children in this language too. He was reasoning about shape and space and enjoying the responsibility of a real dilemma to handle.

It is essential for the adult in such a situation to take the dilemma seriously in order to respect the contribution and make the storytelling environment a valued learning context. If the teacher in this scenario had simply said, 'It's OK, I can squeeze it through the door', it would have been an abuse of her status and an insult to the boy's thinking skills and intelligence.

If we are to initiate young minds into the concepts of global citizenship, cultural diversity, the problems of the erosion of the environment and other issues, we must provide them with believable dilemmas and strong characters. We need to provide genuine experiences for discussion, argument and questioning if we are to extend their thinking skills. As Smith (1992: 42) argues, 'Learning is not something that is done separately from thinking . . . Inferring, concluding, deciding and solving problems are inseparable from learning'.

The whole child

It is impossible to prepare children for all eventualities in a diverse world and so a suitable solution is to enable children to become what Claxton (2000) calls 'toolmakers': 'If we can't give them the tools that we anticipate they are going to need to manage their lives, at least we can try and make them toolmakers. Give them the ability to develop and craft their own tools as and when they meet the challenges. That's learning to learn, or what I call learnacy'.

Claxton suggests we do this through immersion in experience, intuition, intellect, imagination and *creating imaginary worlds*. He also talks about learning temperament, stating the importance of resilience, conviviality and having a playful disposition. 'The evidence is that you are much more able to work creatively with information if I told it to you in a "could be" language rather than a "this is" language. So that having that ability to be playful is one of the most important characteristics of life-long learning'.

As a fundamentally people-based activity, drama is a natural method for the development of 'playfulness' and a 'could be' language. By fostering a playful disposition, the use of imagination and intuition drama encourages conviviality and social confidence. Through exploring the action of the drama in terms of its potential for developing communication, attitudinal and emotional understanding, thinking skills, concepts and knowledge, a dual map of the dramatic and educational learning can be prepared.

When using drama, children willingly engage in contexts where the possibilities are infinite. The story that they create through interactive storytelling, for example, can continue in as many ways as there are children contributing, and more. Children become more willing to make contributions when they realize the malleable nature of the stories. They begin to understand that beyond their own ideas and desires many alternatives exist. Through the exploration of dilemmas, children become aware that there are many different ways of responding to a situation and they see that each response has its own implications. They are learning to look at contexts in all their complexity and to consider action and consequence. More importantly, they learn that they can be the decisive element in a situation.

Children with special educational needs

Initially, some children can find the sense of freedom and ambiguity and the assorted possibilities that drama can offer difficult to manage. This is particularly so if children are used to functioning in a controlled environment, where there are set patterns and routines with little real choice or decision making.

Catherine, an autistic 4-year-old was involved in a story-making session about a birthday party. She was able to relate to the context of a birthday party. This was important for Catherine as it meant she had experiences that she could use to make connections with the imaginary story. She found no difficulty in suspending her disbelief. Her first reaction was to follow the other children, copying and mimicking their actions. This was an entirely appropriate response. She was aware of others, observing them closely, and copying their behaviour so that she was a socially accepted part of the situation. As the drama progressed she held out her hand, as an imaginary cup to be filled with drink and then drank the imaginary contents. She ate the imaginary food. She played 'pass the parcel', receiving and passing the mimed parcel around the circle. She also handed a mimed present to the child who was hosting the party and repeated 'Happy Birthday'.

Catherine responded throughout the drama in an entirely appropriate manner. Her verbal interactions were all repeated from other children, but she was modelling and using language appropriate to the situation. However, in drama sessions where unknown contexts were used Catherine became confused. She found it difficult to isolate moments in time and use language in a creative fashion, although she was able to be expressive with her body and enjoyed using her voice. She was able to copy still images or echo phrases but was unable to give her own response.

Overall, a 'living through' experience using a familiar context was more suitable for Catherine's needs. Although much of her drama work was mimicking, this does not devalue her experience in any way. She needed to model behaviour and language before she was able to make her own contributions. With autistic children such as Catherine, the use of action, gesture and ritual are an initial way of offering the opportunity of an individual response.

As children become more comfortable with the security that drama offers they are able to make contributions that are more positive. They realize that there is no right or wrong answer, just a variety of possibilities. When working in drama, children use contexts that are diverse and changeable, rich with possibilities. Drama does not put children in a false position of control. They are operating within the confines of a situation where they can manage decisions, change and uncertainty. It is their decisions and their actions that make things happen. This is as important for children with special educational needs as for any other child.

Equal opportunities

Children become aware of colour, language, gender and physical differences at a very early age. Research demonstrates that during a child's second year of life they become aware of gender and racial differences (Honig 1983; Roopnarine 1984; Siraj-Blatchford 1993). Children may notice physical disabilities, but research shows that this awareness often develops later (Levitt and Cohen 1976). During a child's second year, as their use of language develops, they learn and use gender labels such as 'boy' and 'girl' and learn the names of colours which they use in the context of skin colour.

By the time they are 3, children may show signs of bias towards others on the grounds of race, gender or ability. They will also explore and establish elements of their own identity, including which aspects of their identity will remain constant – i.e., Will I always be a girl? By the time children are 4 or 5 they display gender-appropriate behaviour, as defined by society's norms, and may use racial reasons for refusing to interact with others different to themselves. They may also be uncomfortable in the presence of, or reject, differently-abled people.

The need for bias to be addressed and challenged is justified when we are presented with such startling evidence. One important thing to remember is that prejudice is negative for all children. It is as negative for children who struggle against prejudice and are oppressed by it as for those who receive privilege or a feeling of superiority due to their class, race, gender or ability. All these children have a distorted view of the world. It is not the differences that cause problems, but how people respond to those differences. We need to empower children, so that they are able to think critically, be problem solvers and have the confidence to speak out when they think that something is unjust.

Addressing bias

In a broad and balanced curriculum, issues regarding equal opportunities and bias need to be addressed, through the environment we provide, through the way we respond to children's comments and questions and through the specific issues we choose to explore with them. By using a drama context and the pretend self, we can offer children exploration and protection, nurturing their inquiring and questioning minds. Challenging bias and prejudice, however, should be part of the school ethos and needs to be integrated across every aspect of a child's life, not just slipped into a 20-minute drama session.

When looking at children's social relationships, Emihovich (1980: 73) found that 'structure and teaching methodology significantly affected the amount and quality of children's interracial peer interactions'. Children form ideas and values not only from what we say, but from what we do *not* say. They are as influenced by our lack of response to situations and by what we omit to provide as they are by our explicit responses and provision. When working with and challenging controversial issues, there is a need to remain developmentally appropriate, yet we must acknowledge that even the very youngest children in our care may be experiencing conflict or discrimination in their daily lives.

Gender

All children will benefit from challenging prejudice and stereotypical attitudes. For example, gender stereotyping eliminates whole areas of experience and results in neither men nor women being adequately prepared for the diversity of modern life. Epstein (1995: 59) suggests:

> It would in these circumstances be astonishing if the vast majority of 3- to 5-year-olds had not inscribed themselves well within the gender to which they had been ascribed. If others constantly interpret them and their world through discourses of gender difference, what else is available to infants as they begin to make sense of the world for themselves?

Issues such as 'costuming', often encouraged by adults, cause hidden conditioning that promotes genderism in a covert way; girls are given nurses' outfits and boys Superman costumes, for example. Girls have prams and dollies, boys play with fast cars and Action Men. There are also issues about the gender identification of certain chosen roles. Boys are more likely to choose the doctor role rather than the nurse or patient/baby role. Research seems to show that boys are less likely to adopt conventionally female-specific roles such as 'mothers', whereas girls will quite happily role play as 'fathers', 'builders', 'hunters', 'vehicle drivers' and other 'male'-orientated parts (Goldman 1998).

If we refuse to address this, maybe because we feel it is inappropriate for an early years curriculum, then we are leaving children to solve difficulties and problems alone. We need to listen to and work from children's questions, concerns and comments. A variety of issues will arise naturally in drama work. During a recent interactive story, on a trip to the moon, a 4-year-old boy was determined that he should 'fly' the rocket because he was a boy. We, the adults involved, had a choice. Were we going to challenge, in an inquiring, non-threatening way, or were we going to re-affirm the view that only boys can be pilots? How would we store that comment and use it to address this child's needs?

Prejudice and difference

We can explore issues around the theme of prejudice through parallel situations. The storybook *Ruby* by Maggie Glen (Glen 1992) tells the story of Ruby the bear, who is a 'second' and therefore inferior because she was made from the wrong-coloured fur. A story such as this can be used in drama work to explore how it feels to be different, or how other people might respond to you because of difference. The feelings and the prejudice remain constant, but the context of a bear in a toy shop offers protection.

As practitioners, we are able to use drama to create contexts that will explore prejudice. We also have to be ready to deal with issues regarding prejudice that naturally arise. Each child will bring to the drama their concerns and interests. Issues will emerge from their everyday lives and from prominent events that are happening in the world.

Education for a pluralist society

Storybooks are a powerful starting point for drama and an ideal medium for exploring cultural, racial and religious differences. It could be said that most books reflect social values and it is our responsibility to ensure that the books we choose reflect a diversity of gender roles, racial and cultural backgrounds, ability, age range and occupations, as well as a variety of family lifestyles and different levels of economic status.

When equipping role play areas, we should think about the gender roles that we are establishing and if the clothing we provide reinforces traditional roles – e.g. a doctor's coat and a nurse's dress. Role play areas should cater for cultural diversity, including a variety of cooking and eating implements, hats, clothing and personal items such as combs and jewellery. Mirrors that children can see into are also important in a role play area. Children should be able to look at themselves and others. Dolls used in role play areas should reflect a diversity of cultures and have a realistic range of skin tones. A balance of male and female dolls should also be offered, with appropriate clothing (e.g. girls need dresses *and* trousers).

Children also need access to various aids used by people with special needs, such as crutches, glasses and wheelchairs. It is often the unfamiliarity of such aids that contributes to prejudice and fear. The role of the adult in supporting the play in the role play area is vital. We must ensure that there is an appropriate variety of gender and cultural roles and that both boys and girls are included.

The special needs of the bilingual child

Most of the children in UK playgroups and classrooms are monolingual – that is to say, they speak only one language. However, bilingual children are on the increase and are operating in two languages: one for school and one for home. Bilingualism should not be seen as a handicap but as a positive asset in a group. As Jago (1999: 165) points out, 'fluency in another language brings not only increased knowledge, but also cultural engagement and extension of thinking. Code-switching provides the bilingual with an additional means of expression'. She also cautions that a lack of recognition of languages in the learning process can confuse very young children who are at 'a critical stage of conceptual development'.

Drama provides an essential learning medium in which monolingual children can be helped to value other languages. For example, during a story-making session with a group of 2- and 3-year-olds that contained several Urdu speakers, the Urdu-speaking carer was asked to take the part of an old lady. She wanted some information from the group but told them she could only speak her native tongue. The Urdu-speaking children moved forward and excitedly began to speak to her. They were able to 'translate' for the others what the old lady was saying. This made them very special in the eyes of their peers who proceeded to ask more questions in English so that they could be translated for the old woman. In these circumstances the bilingual children were seen to be at a great advantage.

The monolingual child whose language is not that of the group has a different set of difficulties but sometimes finds a release through drama. For example, a Polish 5-year-old who was finding the English-speaking environment an alien place, found he could contribute in the story-making. As much of what was being done was visual, he could follow the 'pictures'. The group in the story found themselves unable to climb up a cliff until the Polish child drew a pulley system on a piece of paper. He explained how it worked in Polish and broken English and became an important part of the story.

This form of code-switching not only increases knowledge about language for all the participants but allows a furthering of cultural understanding and a development of thinking.

Drama and specific curriculum areas

It would be difficult to deliver a meaningful programme of study in English without using drama. We have discussed in depth the importance of drama for language learning in Chapter 3. In meeting the objectives of both the National Curriculum and *Early Learning Goals* (DfEE/QCA 1999a) the application of drama is essential. Within the National Curriculum, drama now has a place in the English orders, under Speaking and Listening. However, this by no means recognizes the substantial contribution drama can make towards the education of children. The ambiguity of the drama objectives may also prove baffling for the many practitioners who have little or no drama training.

When looking at the objectives for language and literacy in both curriculum documents, the place of story and narrative is central. Children need to learn about the construction of stories – how stories are introduced, developed and concluded. They are asked to recount the main events of a story in correct sequence. There is no doubt that children need to be immersed in story, with a rich diversity of content and presentation. We have discussed how it is important that children hear oral storytelling and have stories brought to life through puppets and presentation. Children also need to become storytellers themselves and this initially has to be a playful and practical experience.

Children need the opportunity to create stories through using role play areas, puppets, small world play, interactive storytelling and drama activities. It is through being involved in stories and creating stories that children will begin to understand the structure, technicalities and possibilities of them. When working with interactive storytelling children become aware that they can create and influence the story, but also, because they are active participants, they understand the need to make the story absorbing. They pose endless dilemmas and create tension, excitement and fear. Although the story may seem endless and the plot complex, at the end of a session when a story is recalled most children can offer a detailed sequence of events. They remember what happened, how that caused something else to happen. They talk about what they would like to happen next (however, not all children recall in such detail when they have been passive listeners). Through collaboratively creating stories in various contexts, children develop their understanding of story structure, sustain active listening and respond to what they have heard.

However well the formalities of writing are taught, such as spelling and punctuation, we emphasize again that children need something to write *about*. They need opportunities to generate and create imaginative ideas. The role play area is often a good place for writing to begin, offering a context and purpose for writing, whether that be to write a shopping list, or take an order in a café. Children of 5 and 6 years of age are quite capable of using a drama experience to inspire their own writing.

There are many contexts rich with mathematical and scientific possibilities. To bring them into a story, the adult could impose dilemmas such as 'We can only get seven people on the rocket – how are we all going to get to the moon?' This should lead to problem solving, probably involving number recognition and number calculations, and is likely to be far more exciting and meaningful than the average mental maths input! It could also lead to various instances of follow-up work, including formal or emergent recording. We are not proposing that the mathematics curriculum could be delivered solely through drama, but there are possibilities on which to capitalize, giving children the opportunity to use their mathematical skills in interesting and meaningful contexts.

Other areas of the curriculum, such as knowledge and understanding of the world or history and geography, also have aspects that can be successfully delivered through the use of drama. Our example of the science assessment (see p. 74) reveals how different story-based situations can be used to assess or develop children's scientific knowledge.

There are many places of historical interest which now offer schools a 'living through experience', the most popular being a Victorian school day. Within school, the role play area could be transformed into a Victorian kitchen with a range and tin bath. We acknowledge that learning about history can be very abstract, especially for young children. They need a 'hands-on' approach where information is combined with action and artefacts. The practitioner is a vital tool, able to use drama conventions such as teacher in role to adopt the role of somebody from the past in order to give information and answer questions. This can be an engaging way of offering information.

In terms of geography, particularly environmental aspects, drama can also play an important role. The statement of values in 'Curriculum 2000' (DfEE/QCA 1999b) includes a section regarding the environment. There is a growing concern over human treatment of the planet and maintaining a sustainable environment. Drama can be used to create communities where the children adopt various roles from a typical community and the teacher poses environmental problems. The children will learn how their actions affect the environment and find out about various ways of caring for it. Books such as *Giant* (Snape and Snape 1989) and the 'Percy the Parkkeeper' stories (Butterworth 1992) provide strong environmental themes from which important issues about our countryside and planet can be discussed.

Conclusion

Regular opportunities to work with drama will help to foster many of the important components in a 'tool box of learnacy' (Claxton 2000). We are not concerned with providing children with an abundance of prescribed information and answers. Drama is concerned with giving children tools for life, tools with which they can facilitate aspects of their own learning. It develops the thinking skills outlined in Curriculum 2000 (DfEE/QCA 1999b) and the ability to process, reason, enquire, think creatively and evaluate. Through drama, children have the opportunity to work creatively with information. They deal with uncertainty, morality and decision making.

In drama, all worlds are possible. It is for us as practitioners to create imaginary worlds to meet the needs of children, in the hope that a rehearsal for life will produce positive effects in the real world. The learning opportunities that arise from drama are immense and span all the dimensions of a curriculum for young children. We can use drama not only to meet the objectives laid down for us, but also to equip children with the skills and experiences that will contribute towards making them valuable citizens. Drama will 'enable pupils to think creatively and critically, to solve problems and to make a difference for the better' (DfEE/QCA 1999b: 11).

Throughout this chapter we have talked about the need for a curriculum that is not merely subject orientated, but one that feeds and nurtures the whole child – a curriculum broad and balanced in its preparation for what life offers. Adults of the future may find the factual information given to them today will be superseded tomorrow. Factual information can be accessed from other sources. What we need to provide is a wide range of experience that will equip young people with skills to face an uncertain future.

Summary

This chapter has identified:

- the need for a holistic curriculum that develops the whole child, not just subject knowledge;
- the need to prepare children for life in a changing world;
- the importance of developing children as 'toolmakers' and critical thinkers;
- the role of drama in facilitating skills for life and learning;

- the contribution drama can make to specific curriculum areas;
- the need for practitioners to plan for drama, but also to facilitate subsequent learning that arises from the drama;
- the need for practitioners to plan beyond a subject-based curriculum.

6

Performance in the early years

> . . . it must be said that no infant school child will suffer in any
> way or lose one fragment of educational opportunity if it never
> once appears in public throughout the whole of its school life –
> indeed the corollary that all infant children would benefit from
> never appearing in public is very true.
>
> (Way 1967: 281)

Unlike Brian Way, who suggests that early years children 'would benefit
from never appearing in public', we would like to put forward some
reasons why we feel they should. Bolton (1993: 44) also draws attention
to this fact when he suggests:

> DIE [drama-in-education] is concerned with change in understand-
> ing, but it is a mistake to isolate this objective by treating it as a com-
> modity separate from form. I suggest that such tunnel vision leads
> to extreme views of drama as either functional role play or theatre
> 'studies', both skills- and information-based and both in the long run
> doing a disservice to drama as an art.

We see this chapter as having a dual function: initially to investigate the
effect performance might have on young children and whether, as suggested by some, it does them harm. Second, we want to suggest that
through playmaking rather than script-learning from published plays,
children are provided with conceptual knowledge about aesthetic quality.

In order to discover whether performing to an audience was harmful to
young children, we spent some time investigating how early years children
felt about appearing in public. We used their experiences of the Christmas
Nativity play as our guide. During this investigation it became clear that
there is great potential in the use of role play and limited performance as
a means for the non-drama specialist to develop speaking and listening

skills. The National Curriculum requires children to have had a variety of experiences in different types of talk. Categories such as 'narrating' and 'imagining' become more significant if children are using prepared scenes that give the added dimension of a visual image to their ideas. When a child or an adult is being interviewed in role (hot seating) the other children are both audience and participants in the performance.

We are more interested in how the children view performance and the learning potential of such an enterprise rather than the event itself. Children's first encounter with 'performing' is often the Nativity play. From our observations, it is clear that children, on the whole, enjoy participating – singing, moving across the space, playing an instrument in the presence of their peers or parents. Some 4-year-old children made the following comments after their first experience of performance:

'I liked being Gabriel and I would like to be Mary. I liked walking across the hall and I liked standing on the stage.'

'I liked being a shepherd and I liked walking across the hall.'

'I liked our play but I would like to be Mary next time.'

'I liked the play. I liked looking at my mum and dad as well, I liked waving at my mum and dad. I liked the costumes as well. I liked the bit where we had to stand on the block. I would like to be Mary next year because I like wearing long dresses.'

'I liked the play because I like dressing up and I saw my mummy and my daddy and granny and granddad. My favourite bit was me sitting on the block because I like people looking at me. I want to be Rudolph next year because I have my Rudolph things.'

It was clear that these 4-year-olds were happiest when they were actively doing something. They enjoyed the thrill of walking across the acting area to their places and they liked singing the carols and songs with the other children.

When interviewing 5- and 6-year-olds who had the opportunity to speak individual lines or perform as part of choral speaking and singing groups, we began to find evidence of commitment and understanding of the nature of performance. These children seemed to understand that performance is not spontaneous but needs to be practised, and that it requires the appropriate use of space:

'We practised for a long time so we could do it properly.'

'I was a reindeer. It wasn't good for the reindeers because they didn't have enough room.'

There were several references to the event on the day and reactions from parents were an important feature for many of the children:

'My mum said it was very good except for my antlers. They kept falling off!'

'My parents really enjoyed it.'

'I thought I read very well and my mummy and grandma said I was good.'

'I liked our Christmas play. It was called *The Night Before Christmas*. Michael read the book and Joe read the book too. When we were home my mum said, she said to me, it was beautiful.'

Throughout the age ranges, responses to the question 'What did you like about being in the play?' were very similar. The children had enjoyed singing, watching other children's plays, having words (in one instance described as 'hard' words) to say, being watched, being 'on stage', feeling brave, feeling warm with excitement inside, wearing costumes and having mums and dads to watch.

In response to the question 'What didn't you like?' the children's replies included not having enough to do, trying to remember where they were supposed to be and what they had to do, feeling embarrassed about doing things in front of others, too much practising and worries about things going wrong.

Perhaps more revealing were the answers to the question 'Would you like to do it again? If yes, what would you like to be different?' To the first part of the question there was an overwhelming 'yes'. From an adult's point of view more thought-provoking were the responses to the second part of the question. In every age range there were children who expressed a desire to have more to say, and in one case a child wanted to sing by themselves. These children wanted their parts to be longer and more involved:

'I would have liked a bigger part with more to say.'

'I think we should be allowed to do more talking.'

'I would like to sing by myself, not with everyone else.'

It was difficult to ascertain from such young children what they were experiencing when they were given 'acting' parts. Had they been attracted to the 'feelings' of being on stage or were they interested in the 'techniques' of performance? From the answers there seemed to be a mixture of the two. There is always a danger that young children could become 'hooked' on self-projection and that allowing 'show-offs' to dominate a performance could destroy quality work. However, this tendency can be channelled and focused with skilful handling. This prevents such children becoming Slade's (1954) 'bombast, little boasters' in later life. Young children, if encouraged to do so, seem to be interested in getting it right.

Some of the 6-year-old children were interested in the more technical aspects such as working the lights and doing sound effects: 'Could we do the lights next year?'; 'I think we should have had some special noises for the reindeers. I could do that.' Costumes, too, were an important feature: 'I think we should have proper costumes'; 'I liked it because you could get to be someone different and it's fun. You can dress up – I really like that.'

We were beginning to gather evidence that these young children had a developing concept of aesthetic awareness and quality. They knew how 'theatre' worked and they were aware of space, characterization and theatrical effects. They also had a sense of audience behaviour. One of the most revealing statements came from a 5-year-old boy who had become concerned that the parents didn't know how to be an audience because 'they were laughing and smiling in the wrong bits'. When asked why he thought they were doing this his answer was: 'Because we weren't good enough?' This child was clearly able to understand the importance of quality and aesthetic integrity within a performance.

Kitson and Spivey (1997: 20) rightly say that 'We have all seen children barking learned lines at an audience or performing gross mimicry of adult behaviour . . . The answer lies in the quality of the experience that they undergo'. Early years children are capable and skilful enough to perform with conviction and quality. It is often we, the adults, who do not have the trust that they can do so.

Planning for performance

There is probably no escape from the yearly Christmas productions where invariably the 2-, 3- and 4-year-old children perform the Nativity. This event is more about tinsel, pretty costumes and good public relations than a learning experience for the children to enjoy. We suspect this annual occasion is more akin to 'painting by numbers' (or in this case, 'acting by numbers') than a relevant artistic experience. Any dramatic understanding will come about purely by chance as, through lack of time, there is often little attention paid to aesthetic quality. As Kempe (1996: 27) astutely observes, 'The thought of performance in school might, in its most negatively stereotyped form, conjure up images of children stumbling through lines and dropping the baby Jesus in front of parents, teachers and friends who are at once delighted with the effort but scepti-cal of the artistic quality'.

The lack of artistic quality comes from the directed scripts and moves imposed on young children by overworked adults who have neither the time nor sometimes the skill to make the experience meaningful. The regimentation of such occasions can disconcert and discourage young actors, leaving them de-skilled and confused.

Yet, despite this, without any performance opportunities at all, children could be losing valuable openings to acquire any aesthetic conceptions about quality and achievement. As Hornbrook (1991: 71) reminds us, 'the acquisition of any craft and the knowledge that goes with it, requires prac-tice, repetition and direction'.

Children are now much more sophisticated spectators. From birth they have been exposed to creative presentation and technical effects through television and video and they appear to have, from an early age, a strong understanding of performance.

Performance in the home

Parents can play an important part in encouraging children to become familiar at an early age with replaying and repeating their play, even when it was not initially intended for performance or sharing. This example shows how Harriet, an imaginative 2-year-old, with prompting from her mother, shared a story she had created. She had recently been on holiday to Spain by plane, a new experience that had a great impact. Earlier in the day, Harriet had arranged all her soft toys on the bottom of the staircase. They were waiting at the airport and Harriet proceeded to instruct them to get on the plane: 'On you get, on plane'. Her play was very involved and sustained. She gave her toys drinks and entertained them. Unknown to Harriet, her parents were listening to her from upstairs. Her play con-tinued until there was a long period of silence. Her mother called out to her to ask what she was doing. Sitting at the bottom of the stairs sur-rounded by toys, Harriet said: 'Waiting for plane'.

Later in the day, Harriet's mother proudly related the story to some friends who were visiting. Harriet began to replay some of her scenarios and again sat at the bottom of the stairs waiting to be asked what she was doing so she could deliver her punchline: 'Waiting for plane'. All the adults laughed adoringly as her parents had done the first time she said it, and Harriet enjoyed the attention. She delighted in sharing her play and provoking such a pleasing response. She did not understand the humour, but knew that her words could make adults, her audience, laugh.

Children can share their play with their siblings. Much pleasure can be had making plays using favourite fairy-story characters and showing the results to others by appearing from behind the front-room curtains and using them as stage curtains. Small children can be encouraged to share play with puppets, using the back of the sofa as a makeshift stage. Preschool children can start by sharing their play in small groups. The adult can ask 2- and 3-year-old children to show them how they used the role play area that day. What happened? What did they do next?

The main aims of presentation

We need as our starting point to know why we want young children to perform, and for whom. There is a degree of difference between the small group puppet performance given for a few peers in the safety of the home or teaching space and the big end-of-Christmas-term performance given for parents. The main aim of presentation should be the communication of the children's own ideas to others.

There are a variety of possible audiences that include the adults working with a group, a small group of children from another group, the rest of the class, another class, the rest of the school and parents. Opportunities for presentation occur regularly during group time – for example, when one child shows another something they have done. Circle-times and assemblies provide a vehicle for sharing and presenting, and all these occasions give children experience in sharing ideas, developing their drama skills and experimenting with the relationship between being a performer and being a member of an audience.

Performance for young children should evolve from their work in group drama. It is unfair to expect them to perform for a parent audience if they have not had any experience of performing in a safe environment. They can be introduced to presentation through their work in story-making: 'Can Sarah's group show us how their wings work?' allows one group of children to present to another.

Using drama conventions such as still image allows each group to show one another their work; everyone becomes presenters and audience. It is important to introduce this kind of 'showing' in an unthreatening manner. At the nursery stage, 2- and 3-year-old children will not be aware they are being watched. By the time children have reached 5 to 6 years, they can be introduced to the concept of audience and audience behaviour. This also makes children aware of when they are watchers and when they are being watched.

Puppet shows

Puppet shows are a useful introduction as the 'performers' are protected by the anonymity of the puppets they are using. The self-conscious behaviour that is sometimes present in very shy children is often dispelled when they can 'hide' behind the role taken by their puppet.

Transition from drama into presentation

Children who have had exposure to dramatic activity over a period of time find the transition from classroom drama to 'showing' to others much easier. Morgan and Saxton (1987) make the distinction between 'presentation' and 'performance'; the former being more akin to a theatre workshop production or work in progress and the latter to a fully developed production. The first focuses on the makers and their enjoyment of their work and the second on the audience and their satisfaction with the work.

Public showing of work in early years settings should concentrate on the idea of presentation and the children's enjoyment of sharing, rather than expecting the restricted discipline required of a rehearsed performance. This does not mean to say that children need not rehearse or want to do well, but the adults and parents must be sensitive to the needs and learning requirements of their children.

The Christmas play

Very often there is the expectation that the 'Christmas play' be presented in a theatrical manner. Institutions borrow staging and lights and armies of parents are drafted in to make costumes and props. Unless the teacher has had some personal experience in theatrical direction this form of production is very difficult to manage and achieve well. Most adults do not have the background or the time to cope with such problems. There is the danger that young children become swamped with the production and such performances have very little to do with presenting children's work.

We urge adults required to undertake these events to keep it as simple as possible. Allow what is shown to grow from stories you are making with the children. If the Nativity is obligatory we advise you to work with the story over several weeks in your usual drama slot.

You could look at the story through the eyes of the shepherds or the angels, and with the children develop a new approach to the story. Children are quite capable of inventing scenes and working on them. Some relish speaking lines they have made up themselves. Some establishments have used modern stories such as 'Postman Pat' or stories from around the world as an alternative to the Christmas story. It is important to look at the cultural mix of children and not to ignore other faiths and beliefs.

By moving away from the regimented, over-stressful fortnight of rehearsals the Christmas event can become not only enjoyable but also an aesthetic learning experience for the children.

Live performance

Not only should children be encouraged to present their own work, it is also important that they see the work of others. Children's theatre, puppet theatre and theatre-in-education have a long tradition in the UK. Children's theatre groups and puppet theatres visit schools and usually perform fairy stories and folk tales, with the children as the audience. They provide an ideal introduction to the world of the theatrical event that allows children to experience the 'magic' of live performance. Theatre-in-education, on the other hand, offers children the opportunity to be both spectator and participant.

Many schools take advantage of visiting theatre groups and they are a valuable resource. Theatre-in-education companies provide a broad range of work from participatory programmes for a class or small group to large-scale programmes for the whole school. Some of these companies are still supported by local education authorities and you may be able to arrange a visit via your local LEA. It is also worth approaching your local secondary school who may have a theatre-in-education module as part of their drama GCSE. They are often only too pleased to have somewhere to take their finished programme. The local higher education institution might also have students engaged in preparing such programmes.

By being spectators and participants in theatrical events children can be brought face to face with life's joys, dilemmas and tribulations. For example, a local infant department with some trainee teachers had devised a programme based on 'The Princess and the Frog'. The children who participated in the story became totally involved with the characters and their problems. During the final scene when the children had reached the Princess's palace with the Frog and his other fairy story friends, the Frog asks to kiss the Princess and she refuses. The Frog reminds her that she has promised, an agreement she fervently denies. At this point an indignant 5-year-old got to his feet and reprimanded her saying, 'You did.

You did promise.' Turning to the King, the Princess's father, he continued, 'She did, she did promise.' Turning again to the Princess he said, 'You mustn't break your promises.'

Total involvement in this way allows us to hear and see what children really think and believe. The experience had been a very immediate one for all the children and as audience and participants they had an opportunity to explore and develop their own morals, codes of conduct and ideas.

Conclusion

We must not forget that drama is a performing art. It does not require special training or arcane knowledge to participate in it. By encouraging individual ways of thinking, feeling and acting we can inspire our children to become intuitive and sensitive performers.

Summary

In this chapter we have discussed:

- the importance of aesthetic quality in performance;
- the innate ability of young children to understand the nature of performance;
- the difference between presentation and performance;
- the significance of young children being both able to participate in, and be an audience for, live performance.

● ● ● Part 2

Managing dramatic activity

... it is about alternative worlds which involve 'supposing' and 'as if' which lifts players to their highest levels of functioning. This involves being imaginative, original, innovative and creative.

(Bruce 1991: 64)

7

Creating role play areas

> Contrary to some perceptions of T.I.R. [teacher in role], it is
> close to the usual way of working of early years teachers.
> They often use simple role-play with children in the theme
> corner – being a customer in a café or post office – or slip into
> role when doing story time with the children.
>
> (Toye and Prendiville 2000: 24)

Homes, preschool play groups and nursery settings are seldom without some form of 'pretend play' area. These can take the form of cushions piled up under the dining-room table for 1–2-year-olds, to sophisticated plastic or wooden houses in which children can play. But the idea of 'home' corners or role play areas in reception classes, or further up the infant school, has not so much been lost as given a very low priority. Over the last few years, with the pressure of introducing *Desirable Outcomes* (SCAA 1996) and more recently *Early Learning Goals* (DfEE/QCA 1999a), the 'home' play area has often not been regarded as enough of a valuable learning resource to be retained.

Role play, as we have tried to establish in Part 1 of this book, is an essential part of children's personal, social and emotional health as well as a dimension of intellectual growth from the age of 12 months. We include here such activities as the role playing of 'mummies and daddies', keeping house, shopping etc. as well as the more imaginative play of being spacemen, contending with dinosaurs in Jurassic Park or pretending to be Teletubbies. Many of these play activities occur spontaneously, undirected by parents or carers, and are often seen as something children can 'get on with' while parents attend to other domestic tasks or educators concentrate on delivering the National Curriculum.

However, we would like to suggest that parents, carers and early years practitioners should include provision for all aspects of pretend play in their planning. We must think beyond the use of role play as a support for more free time or as an aid to classroom management: keeping children occupied while the adults are engaged elsewhere. There are occasions when this is justifiable – sometimes it is important to allow children to play alone. But there are times when it is beneficial for adults to enter and 'play' with them. If there is no adult interest, children are sent the message that this type of play is not highly valued.

Such adult involvement should include the whole family: Dad, older siblings and Mum. In daycare and educational settings it should comprise all the members of the team, including parent volunteers. Without adult interest and support, children will either stop using role play areas as they were planned to be used, or will not play with any conviction. By entering children's dramatic play in a playful manner, we are able to build up trust and commitment. We are able to add dimensions that children may be unable to sustain for themselves. Our interventions can add the dimensions of persistence and consequence; what children do and say can be challenged, questioned and analysed, not just by the adults but by the children themselves.

Knowing when and how to intervene constructively, without the children feeling you are intruding, requires awareness and effective observation skills. Initially it may be preferable simply to watch the children at play, making some comment as you pass by, avoiding full-scale interventions for a while. You can then assess whether the children are ready to accept you into their make-believe world or not. It is important never to ignore an approach to 'take tea' or 'go shopping', for instance, with the excuse that you are too busy. Over time, it is important to build up children's trust so that they will allow you to enter into their play.

By restricting the play area to only a 'home', with child-sized sink, cooker, refrigerator and such, pretend play is often perceived by both children and adults as very limited. The idea of 'home' confines the activities to domestic situations (and in many cases very British home situations). The renaming of this space as the 'role play' area or 'theme corner' opens up many more possibilities. Having said this, we do feel it is important that 2- and 3-year-olds (and sometimes 4-year-olds) have access to 'home' play materials. It has been our experience that when a role play area has been designated, for example, as a hospital or post office, there are children who colonize other areas in the room to play 'homes'. The book corner is often a favourite space as it offers some seclusion from the rest of the room. There appears to be, for some children (especially those with special needs), a necessity to play in this way over a long period of time.

Creating role play areas

Your choice of activity for the role play area is also important. By providing different types of environment the children are able to explore different kinds of situation. At home you might want a context that encourages communication skills, and you could provide a telephone or preferably two. In group settings, you can supply pencils and paper in the reception area of your 'hospital' or in your 'travel agent' to foster emergent writing; or provide books and magazines in a 'waiting room' to stimulate reading. Making things for a role play area might require the use of maths, design and technology or information technology. Role play areas should be seen as more than dressing-up clothes and the doll's pram.

Children's involvement

Two-year-olds should be encouraged to make dens and other safe places to play. Role play areas for 3–4-year-olds should be discussed with them and at the same time you can also explore how to play there. Children should be allowed to make things for the area, and to arrange the furniture. This gives them ownership of the area. The well-meaning adults who spend their weekend designing and making a new area often find it dismantled by the first children who use it. This is not only disheartening but it is also counter-productive. By involving the children there are many curriculum opportunities for designing and making that you can capitalize upon.

Figure 7.1 shows some of the cross-curricular activities that can be used to enhance the role play area. The children should be encouraged to discuss and make things for the role play. In doing so we allow them to take ownership of the environment that, in turn, stimulates more productive play.

Planning role play

In the home, role play spaces will often appear unplanned whereas educational settings will plan the role play area into their programme. However, parents and educators should encourage and include opportunities for all types of socio-dramatic and thematic-fantasy play. These should not be seen as a hierarchy with solitary socio-dramatic play being the least demanding and thematic-fantasy play being the most sophisticated. All aspects of this type of play should be available for children to engage in if we are to take advantage of the different sorts of cognitive and emotional learning that result from it.

Language

- Make a copy of a newspaper (*The Bear Daily*) which can be used in the role-play.
- Suggest some books for the bookshelves: some for Mr and Mrs Bear and some for Baby Bear (this could lead to discussion about how well bears can read).
- Write out some shopping lists for the Bears to use.
- Write a book of Bear poetry to go on the shelf.

Maths

- Collect different-shaped and different-sized cereal packets (these could be covered and marked 'Porridge').
- Collect different-sized cutlery and crockery (these could be grouped for size in a cupboard in the house).
- Find some different-sized furniture and arrange at a table in order of height.
- Find different-sized tinned food and group in threes.

Science

- Experiment with oats and other grains to see which makes the best porridge.
- Make a list of the plants and animals to be found near the Bears' house.
- Put up a list of poisonous berries and plants that Baby Bear musn't eat.
- Plant some seeds to grow house plants for the Bears' house (they can be watered by children playing in the house).

History

- Discuss whether the Bears' house is old or new: if it is old, how will it look? If it is new, how will it look?
- Make a book of photographs showing the Bears' relations: Grandma Bear, Grandpa Bear, Great Grandma, Great Grandpa (this could lead to discussion on clothes and how they've changed).
- Write some stories in legend form about great Bears of the past, for the bookshelf.

Geography

- Discuss the physical surroundings outside the house: is there a pond or a lake in the forest? Is the house built on a hill or in a valley?
- Find out how to use a compass for the Bears to use on their walks.
- Draw a pictorial map of the forest showing the paths which the Bears can use. Have it in the house for consultation (find a way of folding it for convenience).

Design and technology

- Design a burglar alarm for the Bears' house.
- Design a front door bell for the Bears' house.

Art

- Paint some portraits of the Bears for the walls of the house.
- Make a painting in the style of a famous painter that the Bears could have on their walls.
- Draw a scene of what the Bears can see through their window. Stick it on the wall with a window frame made from paper over the top.

Music

- Compose some Bear music and tape it. It can be played on a tape-recorder in the Bears' house.

Teacher intervention

Children are allowed to play in role using all the things created for the house (they will create the stories). The teacher could intervene in the following roles:

- As a policewoman who interviews the Bears after Goldilocks escapes.
- As Goldilocks's mother who has come to apologise.
- As a property developer who wants to buy the forest for a housing development.
- As a reporter from *The Bear Daily*.
- As one of the Bears giving some children the chance to visit the house in other roles (all these exchanges will give opportunities for talk, sharing opinions and ideas, investigating, reporting and describing events, sharing feelings and listening to others).

Figure 7.1 Cross-curricular activities linked to a 'Three Bears' role-play area

Socio-dramatic play (solitary)

To engage in this kind of play the solitary child needs to have available:

- a collection of domestic utensils: sweepers, cleaning equipment, saucepans, pots with lids, pans, woks, rice boilers, food in bags and tins from different countries;
- dolls (preferably of all skin types);
- a variety of soft toys;
- a doll's pram;
- a sling for carrying the baby.

This type of play will take place anywhere in the room or outside if available. You might observe, for an example, a solitary child pushing a pram around the room talking to the doll or other soft toy inside. He or she will be treating the doll as a baby. A child, on his or her own, might be observed making a meal, cleaning the house or some other domestic chore, and this 'work' is often accompanied by humming or singing quietly.

Socio-dramatic play (with partner/s)

This type of 'role play' will be recognized immediately by early years practitioners: two or more children combining together in different kinds of 'domestic' play. There is often a leader who will be directing and narrating for the others. The leadership role can change quite frequently but the play remains 'domestic'.

The following are examples of the type of pretend play area that will encourage socio-dramatic play:

- a supermarket (items for sale should include a cultural mix);
- a café (food on sale should reflect a range of nationalities);
- a shoe shop (include footwear from different countries);
- a newsagent/sweet shop (if you use real newspapers, try to find some written in other languages);
- a travel agent (include brochures for Africa, South America, Australia and the Far and Middle East, not just European or American destinations);
- an estate agent;
- an optician;
- a doctor's surgery (encourage both boys and girls to play the doctor role; boys should also be encouraged to be 'nurses').

The different contexts offered will give opportunities for different kinds of talk and learning. The doctor's surgery, for example, could have a reception desk and telephone because you want to encourage discussion, the giving of clear and simple explanations, and reasons for actions. The surgery waiting room could have magazines to encourage reading. Cards with numbers for patients so they know whose turn it is to see the doctor will help children with number recognition and number ordering. Writing equipment could be available in the reception area to practise writing skills. The environment chosen might require money to be used. The introduction of place-specific equipment and materials such as white coats, stethoscopes and first-aid kits helps to locate the environment.

Socio-dramatic play (with adults)

The context is similar to the above but now has adult intervention as its focus. Each intervention by an adult varies the learning opportunities and the possible learning outcomes. For example, by entering the 'supermarket' in role as a customer you could:

- ask the assistants where you might find various items on the shelves (encouraging discussion on sorting and ordering);
- find you have not enough money at the checkout and have to make choices about what you leave behind (encouraging discussion about costs and expense);
- complain that some of the items on the shelves are past their use-by-date (encouraging discussion about the health and safety of food).

In the café, you could take on the role of:

- someone in a hurry who wants something to eat very quickly (encouraging discussion about food nutrition);
- someone who complains about the food (encouraging the handling of potentially difficult situations);
- someone who is a vegetarian and wants to know which of the items on the menu contain no meat or animal products (encouraging discussion about the content of food).

In the shoe shop:

- you are a customer who wants a special pair of shoes for a wedding but they must match your wedding outfit (encouraging discussion about style and fashion);
- you have brought back a pair of shoes because they won't fit (encouraging discussion about sizing);
- you want the shop assistants to recommend a pair of shoes that you can

wear on holiday for walking (encouraging discussion about the different varieties of shoes).

In the optician's:

- you want your eyes tested using the letter card (encouraging discussion of the alphabet);
- you want the optician to recommend some new frames for your small child (encouraging explaining abilities);
- you want the optician to recommend some new frames for you (encouraging talk about personal choice).

In the travel agent:

- you are a customer who wants an exotic holiday (encouraging talk about different places in the world);
- you want the assistant to tell you how a holiday by the sea would be different from a holiday in the countryside (encouraging talk of comparison and difference);
- you are new to foreign travel and want to know the means of transport to different places (encouraging talk about different types of transport).

No adult intervention should last for more than a few minutes or so. The play is for the children and the adult's role is to provide a model for effective talk and discussion. The role as a customer in the travel agent might find you flicking through a brochure and saying to the child in their role as assistant, 'That looks a lovely place. I would love to go there. What can you tell me about it?'

Once we join the children at play and adopt a role within their make-believe, we can both initiate and respond in order to facilitate learning. Each adult intervention varies the learning opportunities and the possible learning outcomes. Intervention is particularly effective if the adult identifies and utilizes learning opportunities that arise naturally and are offered by the children themselves. It is important for children to feel some ownership of the exchanges and that their contributions to the play are taken seriously and are valued.

The adult may enter the discourse as the customer but must treat the 'travel agent' with the same respect as if it were real life. This will help to develop the shared fiction in a more public way, as other children could overhear the conversation and be encouraged to join in. The adult's intervention will also help the child in the part of the travel agent to become more committed to their role. By using this approach we are able implicitly to signal to the children that we value their dramatic play. We indicate it is important to us and is a respected form of activity.

As we have recommended previously, be careful about the use of the direct question. It is more helpful to the child if you begin the conversation with phrases, similar to ones you would make to adults before asking a question. These could include, 'Excuse me, I wonder if you could help me?' or 'I don't like to bother you but could you tell me where I might find . . . ?' This receives a much more positive response from children.

As an example, the following exchange was described by a trainee teacher in a class of 5- and 6-year-olds who, in role as a customer, asked for help looking for a suitable holiday:

> *Adult:* I wonder if you could help me? I was hoping to go to Switzerland for a holiday.
> [Sandra begins to look through the brochure.]
> *Adult:* I think Switzerland begins with an 'S'.
> [Sandra continues to look.]
> *Adult:* Oh look, there it is.
> *Sandra:* That looks nice.
> *Adult:* I hope so. Could I book?
> *Sandra:* I'll ring them.

She 'telephoned' Switzerland to make the booking. There followed a conversation about rooms and travel. The adult finally asked Sandra to write down the telephone conversation to Switzerland so that she would not forget it. Times, dates and transport arrangements also take on significance within the context of the play. Such adult and child exchanges probably take less than five minutes but allow the adult to observe carefully what is being said and done.

By entering children's dramatic play in this small way we are able to build up trust and commitment which can be used later when we embark on bigger group or whole-class drama activities. It is only when children are able and willing to accept an adult into their imaginary play situation or environment, and are able to sustain the make-believe verbally and non-verbally, that they will accept us taking on roles within the dramatic situation.

Thematic-fantasy play (solitary)

To encourage thematic-fantasy play the solitary child needs to have available:

- a collection of soft toys;
- a collection of 'small world' toys such as Lego;

- a selection of rod or glove puppets;
- a puppet theatre (if available);
- a box of different materials for dressing up.

This type of play is often 'external': Objects, toys or puppets play out the story with the child as narrator and actor.

Thematic-fantasy play (with partner/s)

This play activity is very similar to the above but more than one child now takes ownership of the story. There may be one or more narrators and different voices are used to distinguish the characters. The pair or group may dress up and act out the characters themselves without the projection through an inanimate toy or object. They will use both verbal and non-verbal actions to maintain the story.

This type of play can be quite disruptive to a home or classroom. The children often 'travel' from the designated role play area to different locations in the room to make their story more interesting. As parents, carers and practitioners we must find ways of being tolerant to this form of activity as it is a very important part of cognitive and imaginative development. If we are to encourage our children to be 'playful' with ideas we must let them experiment with being 'playful' through play.

To encourage thematic-fantasy play the role play areas should not represent familiar locations but should reflect 'all possible worlds'. For example:

- places that take children back in time, such as castles, sailing ships, pirate ships, old houses;
- time-travel settings, such as a spaceship or a time machine;
- fairy-story places, such as the Three Little Pigs' brick house, Little Red Riding Hood's cottage, Cinderella's kitchen or the Seven Dwarfs' house;
- places of the imagination, such as the all-green room, the upside down room, the room of dreams, the house of the magic key.

Thematic-fantasy play (with adults)

This will be fully explored in the following chapter on interactive story-making.

Conclusion

We must keep in mind as we plan for role play in the classroom that there is a distinction between socio-dramatic play and thematic-fantasy play. The script-based socio-dramatic play develops language and communication skills and is important in helping to establish children's understanding of their gender and cultural identity. Thematic-fantasy play develops narrative thinking and children's imagination. It also allows them to recognize and reconcile emotional tensions and universal truths. What we choose to provide for our children will determine the learning opportunities we can exploit.

Summary

This chapter has shown that:

- role play areas are important for all ages in the early years;
- role play areas are significant for both cognitive and emotional development;
- both socio-dramatic and thematic-fantasy play should be planned and provided;
- adult interest and intervention is essential to expand learning.

8

Interactive story-making (thematic-fantasy play with adults)

... where drama and role-play were used effectively there
appeared to be 'better overall standards in literacy'.

(Ofsted 1994: 8)

If drama activity is about anything, it is about the learning and turning-
points in life. Such moments can cause the participants to reflect on their
actions and to rethink some of their ideas from within a safe environment.
To sustain the action the players have to use their knowledge, both factual
and subjective, and they will be introduced to new material, both factual
and objective, which they must use to help them solve problems and take
decisions. This is where parents, carers and early years practitioners play
such a crucial role. As Readman and Lamont (1994: 16) reflect, 'It is the
responsibility of the teacher to: – resist any assumptions about the kind of
role(s) children might adopt; select content areas which reflect genuine
cultural diversity; enable children to adopt roles which challenge any
stereotypes; offer children opportunities to work collaboratively'.

In this chapter we shall outline some ways in which drama, in the form
of interactive story-making, can be used as an effective learning medium
in the early years. We will give some examples of useful stimuli and show
how the original stimulus can be developed. In doing so, we hope to provide parents and early years educators with a strong rationale for including thematic-fantasy play with adults as a learning medium and to allay
fears about using this form of dramatic activity.

The use of fictional contexts puts children in control by utilizing their
existing language, experience, motivations and interests. At the same time,
we can intervene to provide fresh ways of looking at things from the

children's existing experience. These opportunities provide us with a wide range of potential contexts otherwise unavailable.

Through the creation of a fictional world, children are given the opportunity of being who they like, where they like, when they like and of saying what they like. For example, as an introduction to environmental issues, they could enter a fictional world, as themselves, that looked at how to clean up their village. They might be mice trying to reach the moon in order to see whether it is really made of cheese. They could be a group of servants worried about the disappearance of Snow White or, alternatively, farmers trying to work out how you can transfer milk from one milk tanker to another.

Why interactive story-making is important in the early years

Interactive story-making is about giving children experience of imagined events. This takes us into the realm of narrative and creative, imaginative thinking. As we have already identified, role play is a stage of progression within the natural development of children's play. We have also discussed how thematic-fantasy play requires a different form of thinking from socio-dramatic play. By working in the narrative mode that Vygotsky (1978) describes as the highest level of thought, young children have access to Bruner's (1986) 'all possible worlds'.

However, you can keep the stories you are making fully in the real world where all the actions will be controlled by 'natural laws'. Here we are dealing with the paradigmatic mode of thinking that requires the ability to be logical, sequential and analytical. In this kind of story-making there will be a storyline and a resolution, whereas socio-dramatic play with adults, in the main, deals with a single event such as being a customer with a problem in the supermarket. During these more sustained stories you might discuss the environment, design and technology, science or citizenship and so forth.

We describe these two forms as 'home' and 'away' stories. Home stories are those that remain in the real world and take their scripts from real-life situations, whereas 'away' stories inhabit the world of the fairytale and the imagination. In 'home' stories life experience and factual knowledge are applied in an active way, frequently providing a genuine 'need to know'. 'Away' stories encourage imaginative and creative thinking which can transport children into their wildest dreams.

The main features of home stories are:

• Although a fiction, all that occurs is *based* in reality. All activities are controlled by natural laws (magic cannot be used to solve problems).

- They remain in or around the opening environment, which can be inside or outside locations – e.g. schools, playgrounds, shops, offices, the seaside, gardens, farms, zoos, etc.
- They are a useful medium to build stories around topic work and cross-curricular themes.

The main features of away stories are:

- They are based in imaginative experience where all worlds are possible (changes in physical shape and the use of magical powers etc. can be used to solve problems).
- They usually have the feel of fairy stories.
- They usually involve travel far away from the original location to, e.g. distant countries, under the sea, a future world, a make-believe place, etc.
- Travel is often arduous with many adventures and mishaps along the way.
- They allow for the creation of an idealized world.

Making the contract

For some children, there is a fine line between their imaginative worlds and their perception of reality. For this reason, the making of a contract is a vital part of the negotiation process. All participants must agree to take part and share the same action. This is the same for both home and away stories.

Adults must be careful never to begin in role without telling the children that they are doing so. We have witnessed interventions that do not warn the children that an adult has gone into a role. Without an opening statement such as 'What story shall we make today?' or 'We are going to make a story together' to inform children of our intentions, they can become very confused. It is important that children and adults are always aware that they are playing make-believe and that the story can stop.

Direction by adults

Having joined with the children in their story and adopted a role within their make-believe, we can both initiate and/or respond in order to facilitate learning. It is particularly effective if the adult identifies and utilizes learning opportunities that arise naturally and are offered by the children themselves. Children need to feel some ownership of the story and that the contributions they make to the dramatic play are valued.

We have already discussed how, by having to express their feelings, their thinking and their actions to each other, drama causes children to communicate in a meaningful way and to think more deeply about the consequences of their actions. The random 'play' shooting of the playground, for instance, can be challenged – shooting hurts people and this can be explored. Also, by needing to interpret the actions of others, often in unfamiliar ways, and by having the opportunity to replay, change and reflect upon different parts of the action, drama allows children to have new experiences and to test out their reactions in a safe environment.

Using improvisation as the medium for dramatic activity

Interactive stories use both dialogue and non-verbal action, which are constructed as the story proceeds. The talk and actions will be similar to ordinary conversations and actions in real life, but they are taking place in a fictional environment. There is no pre-written script and children do not mime to narration unless such a strategy is used to move the story forward. The role of the adult is to manage and evaluate the dialogue and non-verbal action. In this way, we can take advantage of the greatest learning potential and explore curriculum, emotional and moral matters.

Planning interactive story-making

It is important to capture the children's imagination by giving them a powerful dilemma (tension and suspense) from which they can build belief; in other words something must happen to engage their interest. The children need to be able to enter the story 'as if' it were real. They must have a common willingness to suspend disbelief. Figure 8.1 shows how both home and away stories follow the same core format. The children engaged in the story will need to know where they are, who they are and what they are doing at the start of the story and while it is taking place. As the story progresses they will need experience of how to face dilemmas, how to set and solve problems and how to make decisions. The end of the story can be delayed. We have known stories that have lasted several weeks before a true resolution is found, and others that have taken as little as 20 minutes to be completed.

The adult guides the children to and through the complications they meet on the way. Either the adults or the children can introduce complications. If, however, there is a certain concept or aspect of the story the adult wishes the children to consider, then the adult should introduce the

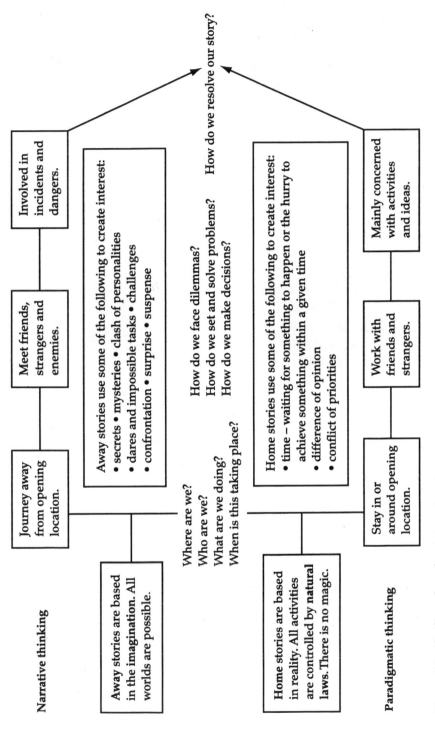

Figure 8.1 Outline plan of an interactive story

complication which leads to discussion as required. Away stories have a habit of moving very fast and it is the responsibility of the adult to keep some focus on the storyline, however unlikely the plot seems to be. Children become confused if the storyline is too fragmented, but on the other hand they lose interest if adults change the story to suit an adult agenda.

Choosing the starting-point

Although we use published and well-known stories as sources for inspiration, we do not follow the storyline and act out the story. We use well-known children's stories, poems and nursery rhymes as useful resources with which to make strong starting-points.

We choose material that contains interesting settings, lively characters and a strong narrative or ideas that capture our imagination and which we think will inspire stories from our children. We have found the following stories, both old and modern versions, to be effective springboards for interactive story-making:

- 'The Three Little Pigs'
- 'Jack and the Beanstalk'
- 'The Princess and the Frog'
- 'The Gingerbread Man'
- 'Snow White and the Seven Dwarfs'
- 'The Elves and the Shoemaker'

Choosing stories with few characters such as 'The Three Little Pigs' would appear to have difficulties if your group is large. However, by making the children the friends of the pigs with you in role as the pigs' mother who is desperate to find them, the story can work very well. Most interactive stories are not driven by a main character. They are more about righting wrongs, finding people, taking people home, fighting enemies and going on quests. The characters, therefore, can be universal types such as villagers, friends, animals, birds, people who know how to fly, experts in different fields and so on.

Picture books and stories with multicultural themes also make excellent beginnings for interactive stories. Some of our favourites are *After the Storm* by Nick Butterworth (1992), *Five Mice and the Moon* by Joyce Dunbar (1990), *Giant* by Juliet and Charles Snape (1989) and *Rama and the Demon King* by Jessica Souhami (1998).

After the Storm begins, not surprisingly, after a storm where a tree which is the home to many animals has blown down. We have used this beginning often with different groups of 2-, 3- and 4-year-olds. Each time we play it, the children involved make different journeys to find a new home. The scariest involved the group trying to pass through a wood which contained wolves with red eyes! This is a useful text to use with groups who find working together difficult. There is much opportunity here for sharing and caring.

Five Mice and the Moon begins with five mice discussing whether the moon is made of cheese and how they could reach it to find out. This storyline is a useful one for exploring gender issues. Discussion and action using the beginning idea of getting to the moon invariably leads to talk about construction involving mathematical problems and those of design and technology. This scenario needs careful handling as it can become male-dominated. If the group decide to make a rocket, the boys have a tendency to assume roles as the builders and pilots. Hence it is such a good vehicle for the discussion of stereotypes.

Giant provides an effective introduction to environment issues. We have used this story as a follow-up after creating our own story about a land that has lost all its trees and greenery. By discussing the children's story and that in *Giant* we can draw parallels between the two.

The ancient Indian tale of *Rama and the Demon King*, an important story because of its relation to Diwali, celebrated by Hindus, is a very difficult and complex story for young children. This relatively simple version can be read as preparation for children's own story-making of ancient tales in which good overcomes evil.

Identifying learning areas

Having selected the context it is worth identifying some of the learning areas that might be explored as the story develops. For home stories we need to look at more curriculum-based learning. Stories set in woods or the outdoors, for example, might lead to environmental issues or aspects of geography being addressed; stories set indoors might provide a background for work in science or maths; whereas stories set long ago might produce some interesting insight into history.

Away stories on the other hand are an excellent vehicle for exploring universal ideas such as:

- How do we find out what people are like?
- How do we deal with people who are different?
- How do we deal with the things that frighten us?
- How do we cope with bullies and people who seem more powerful than us?

- How do we cope when things go wrong?
- How can we become more independent?

First attempts at interactive story-making

Children of 2, 3 and 4 years, and those with special educational needs, can find continuous improvisation for long periods of time a challenge. Very bright children can become frustrated with the lack of action and sometimes follow their own agenda and storylines, thereby fragmenting the group. Those with learning difficulties can become confused if the dialogue and action move away from their known experiences.

While children and adults are learning the rules, the initial attempts at interactive story-making can be difficult. It is important to persist in the early stages and not give up trying because children do not respond in the way we would like. The beginning of the 'castle' story related in Chapter 4 shows the rewards if we persevere.

Defining the space

Interactive story-making is best undertaken in the space most familiar to the children. At home, the living room is usually big enough if chairs and sofas are moved out of the way. In other settings, the assembly hall is often too big and impersonal. It is better to clear a space within children's normal working environment and tell them this is going to be their story-making space for today. If you have to use the hall because your working space is too small, limit the space in which children are allowed to work by defining a space in the middle of the room with gym mats or benches. The children should be told that the story only takes place in this special area and if they go outside the story will stop. This helps to keep the children interested and aids the adult with control.

Starting and stopping the action

It is a good idea to introduce the children to some form of signals to indicate when everyone is in the story and when the story finishes. Some adults use items of clothing to show when they are in or out of the story. You can use words or phrases such as 'action' and 'freeze', or 'is everybody ready to begin?' and 'we are finishing now'.

Interactive story-making using a nursery rhyme as a stimulus

In this section we describe a lesson which uses a nursery rhyme as a starting-point, and show how 2- and 3-year-old children can be engaged in interactive story-making for the first time. One adult should be in overall control and should steer the ideas that are offered. Even parents using interactive story-making with a small group of children at home might find working with a friend as support more productive.

In educational settings, where adults are working with larger groups, as much adult support as possible is essential if children are going to have a meaningful experience. Many parents delight in an invitation to join the story-making. They can make an invaluable contribution to these sessions, not only as an extra adult, but as an experienced listener. Interactive story-making is enhanced when children have enough adults with whom they can share their ideas.

The nursery rhyme used goes like this:

There was an old woman tossed up in a basket,
Seventeen times as high as the moon;
Where she was going I couldn't but ask it,
For in her hand she carried a broom.
Old woman, old woman, old woman, quoth I,
Where are you going to up so high?
To brush the cobwebs off the sky!
May I go with you? Aye, by-and-by.

Learning objectives

- to develop belief in a fictional context by engaging children in an enjoyable drama experience;
- to work as part of a group or class, taking turns and sharing fairly, understanding that there need to be agreed values and codes of behaviour for groups of people, both adults and children, to work together harmoniously;
- to use language to imagine and create roles and experiences;
- to express and communicate the children's ideas, thoughts and feelings.

Procedure

1 Ask the children to sit in a circle. Explain to them that we are going to make a story together. In the story we can be different people and go to different places using our imagination.

2 Tell the children that the adults will be in the story too. Model how the adults will go into role (teacher in role) and how the adults come out of role. (You can use a piece of clothing or a hat when in role and take it off when you are not. Alternatively you can just change the tone and quality of your voice to show the difference.) It is important that the children feel safe.

3 Tell the children the story includes a basket, a broom and a shawl, and show them these objects. (These props will not be used to make the story. They are only used in the beginning as visual concrete artefacts to focus children's attention and get them interested in the story. After you have used the props put them outside the area.)

4 Explain to the children that when the story begins they are going to be helpers and you are going to be a little girl who has a problem. This little girl will need their help.

5 In role as the little girl (you are now a teacher in role) enter the area. Explain to the children that you have lost Granny. Granny told you that she was going up in her basket to sweep the cobwebs off the sky. Your granny has not returned but you found her basket, broom and shawl which had fallen from the sky. Ask the children how they can help.

6 Listen to children's answers. As they will be unused to talking to a teacher in role, if necessary use prompts such as:

'I've never been up in the sky. I have no idea what it is like.'
'Granny says it's very cold in the sky. I don't know what to wear.'
'I don't know how to make Granny's basket fly – can you help me?'
'I have no idea where I should look.'

Hopefully, the children will make suggestions. It is important that you choose a suggestion that comes from the children. Take time to prepare for the journey. You can send them home to tell their mum where they are going. They can pack something to eat for the journey etc.

It has been our experience that making the basket fly can take some time. You have to work out how everyone is to get inside and how many people it will take. On one occasion the children build a space rocket because the basket was too small for everyone. Do not rush through this stage or make the children fly the way you want. It must be their choice. They need to know you are in *their* story and not the other way round.

Give the children time to answer the questions. Be prepared for silences to give them thinking time. Take the beginning slowly – avoid the story moving too fast.

7 Start to make things or collect things. Act this out in a non-verbal way. Children should move around, building and making, with the adults joining in. This is a good time to talk with the 'workers'. Ask them to

show you what to do. Get them to teach you and make them the experts.

8 As the story progresses, create tension by working against time. Granny cannot stay in the sky too long – she could freeze.

'I hope we can find her in time. She won't be able to stay in the sky too long. She'll get really cold.'

Often the children will introduce a tension of their own. They will make something happen. The adults must use this tension and guide it. Children often find something else that belongs to Granny. They get a message from somewhere or the basket/rocket won't fly and you need experts who can put it right.

This stage of the process provides the adults with opportunities to test knowledge or give new knowledge by setting and solving problems. You tried everything but the basket still does not fly. You suddenly become frightened at the thought of going into the sky. You are afraid and you ask the children to help.

9 If the children suggest landing on the moon or another planet, spend time exploring it and looking for clues. Here children may introduce their own subsidiary character but if they don't, introduce a second adult role – 'Man in the moon' or the sole survivor of a spaceship who *either* has been looking after Granny because she is hurt and you need to find a way of getting her home; *or* has captured Granny, who was trespassing, and you will need to negotiate for her release. You can prime your adult helpers beforehand so that they are not taken unawares.

10 End the story by bringing Granny home by whatever method the children choose.

11 You in role as the little girl invite everyone to Granny's house for a party to thank them.

12 Finish the session out of role, back in a circle by reading and teaching the group the nursery rhyme.

Assessment opportunities

- to observe the children who contribute and those who stand aside;
- to observe whether there is an increase in the length of responses;
- to assess the difference in response if children are given thinking time.

This story takes from 20 minutes to an hour depending on the children's interest. You could split it into two sessions of 20–30 minutes each:

- first session – getting into the sky;
- second session – finding Granny.

Dealing with complications

Complications are important as they are the driving force of any story. If the story is to be successful, something must happen to create tension and conflict. During interactive story-making there are occasions when the children overwhelm you with complications. As they begin to realize that they are managing what happens, they will contribute complications in swift succession. It is important at these moments for the adults not to dismiss ideas but to channel them through the use of controls.

Using controls

To keep a story focused, controls can be used to concentrate children's attention. Controls can also be used to create a change in atmosphere. The use of tests such as 'Who can be the quietest?', 'Who is the most sharp-eyed?' or 'Who is the most sensible?' can help to calm a group that is becoming overexcited.

For a group that has become very distracted the introduction of a ritual such as a meeting, a party or a wedding can bring them together. Children can also be brought back together by forming magic circles, passing a squeeze around the ring, everyone hiding, everyone sleeping or any other communal activity which requires everyone's cooperation. See also the use of dramatic conventions, described in the next chapter.

Using reflection

Children of 2, 3 and 4 years will be very concerned with the narrative they are making and will find frequent stopping and starting difficult to manage. It is possible, without losing sense of the plot, to pause awhile within the story to look at what is happening. For example, everyone could sit down when they get to the 'moon' to eat the food they have brought with them. During such episodes the adults can talk with the children about the journey, what they think will happen next and how everyone will get home.

Such opportunities allow the adults to talk with the children about such things as respecting other people's property, acting towards each other in a considerate way, how we might treat people when we come across them or helping others less fortunate than ourselves. These reflections often show themselves later in the plot when any of these events are experienced. This can be observed when children remind each other to look after the environment or treat those less fortunate in a different way.

Resolving the story

The ending of a story should be as significant as the beginning. Young children should leave their stories with a sense of completion and fulfilment; with a feeling of a job well done. These should be stories that could be shared again between themselves or with other children – stories that will be remembered for a long time.

It is important therefore to plan the end as much as the beginning so that the stories finish with some communal activity that brings the whole story together. As in our nursery rhyme story everyone is invited to a party to thank them for their kindness and celebrate Granny's homecoming.

Using stories for home-made books

Stories that a class makes together can be made into story books for bedtime or the book corner. Each child illustrates a part of the story and everyone is asked to remember a part of the story to go into the book. It is sometimes enjoyable to share these stories several weeks later to remind the children of what they did.

Conclusion

Initially it will take time for both children and adults to work together to achieve successful story-making. This activity should not be seen as voluntary, to be abandoned because it appears too difficult to handle. Physical education can be difficult for both adults and children until rules are established, but there is no question that it should be optional. Interactive story-making provides opportunities for children to develop both their paradigmatic thinking and their narrative thinking, without which their education will be the poorer.

Summary

This chapter has shown that:

- interactive story-making requires commitment from both adults and children;
- children should feel empowered by the process;
- children should be directed not led by adults;
- time should be given to building up communal skills.

9

Using dramatic conventions

What are dramatic conventions?

Dramatic conventions are structuring or shaping devices that we can employ to focus children's attention on the variety of questions, events, issues and concepts that arise within a drama story. They have names such as teacher in role, hot seating and still image. We can use these devices to isolate, freeze or focus on moments in the action, which we can then explore with the children. This provides us with further learning opportunities that we might otherwise neglect.

Many of the dramatic conventions used in schools with junior pupils play with time and are therefore difficult to employ with much younger children. Time is a difficult concept and moving backwards and forwards through time can be confusing for the very young. They like to create never-ending stories, which take place in the here and now. Two- and 3-year-olds have an insatiable desire to pose and solve fresh problems or dilemmas. They enjoy a 'living through' experience where time is only played with at their convenience, usually so that the story can progress. Although we will show how simplified versions can be introduced to preschool children, the conventions we recommend here are more suitable for use with 4-, 5- and 6-year-olds.

When a story is in its early stages, dramatic conventions are initially used to establish the content and form, helping to build aspects of plot, character, issues and events that will become the focus as the work develops. As the major elements of content and form emerge, drama conventions are employed to deepen understanding of the story, and commitment to it.

Progression from interactive story-making to the use of dramatic conventions to explore stories

Interactive story-making, as described in the last chapter, is the most effective form of drama for children between 2, 3 and 4 years. By the time children reach 5 and 6 years, they should not only be making their own stories but also exploring well-known and published stories. At this stage, we need to slow down the action and punctuate events through the use of dramatic conventions. Children need to be taught to 'stand aside' from the action and reflect on events, characters and motivations.

For instance, during the exciting, frightening or significant moments of a story we might ask the children to freeze what they are doing and make a frozen picture (still image). While they remain frozen, we might ask them to share what they were thinking as this event happened (thought-tracking). From the still image we might unfreeze the picture to see what might happen next (living pictures).

To find out more about their character, children can interview their peers who have created a significant role (hot seating). The adult can adopt a particular role (teacher in role) to introduce new characters to the story. Using teacher in role allows us to play with status. The adults can choose roles, such as the new servant, someone who needs experts in flying or someone who needs to be shown how to read their map through the wood. In this way, the children are given the opportunity to be more knowledgeable than the adults. By placing children in this higher position, we are making them into experts (mantle of the expert).

Introducing dramatic conventions to preschool children

Children from about the age of 2–3 years can be introduced to the use of simple versions of dramatic conventions such as teacher in role, thought-tracking and mantle of the expert. Introducing dramatic conventions to very young children should be seen as a gradual process. With the 2- and 3-year-olds, we might use some of the conventions within an interactive story-making session but we would not give them a name.

For example, a simple form of hot seating can be used if you want preschool children to meet a new character. The adult will always be in the hot seat for these occasions. The other adults support the children and help them ask questions. In a recent story with 2–3-year-olds, we were trying to help 'Old Bear' who was stuck on the top shelf in the playroom. In order to get him down, we needed to know whether he could move or climb, and so forth. We asked the children to talk to Old Bear. By calling the children into a circle, without breaking the story, the adult in role as Old Bear (teacher in role) sat in the middle. The children, helped by the adults, asked him questions: 'How long have you been there?'; 'Are you hurt?'; 'Are you sad?' Following the interview, or 'hot seat', that only lasted a few minutes, we continued our story.

Thought-tracking can be used in a similar way. Following the discovery of the damage to their tree home 'after the storm', the children were collecting their belongings that had been blown about the wood. Lindsay, a 3-year-old, came to an adult with her hands closed around an imaginary egg:

Lindsay	[in a whisper]: This egg belongs to Mrs Robin.
Adult:	Look everyone, Lindsay has found an egg belonging to Mrs Robin. What shall we do?
Several voices:	Find her.

This incident gave us the opportunity to think about how people might feel if they lost something. We gathered all the 12 children into a ring. As we passed the egg from hand to hand, we asked each child to say what they thought Mrs Robin would be feeling: 'Sad'; 'Unhappy'; 'She's out looking'; 'We mustn't break it'; and so on. Without breaking the spell cast by this activity, we carefully put the egg in a 'basket' to carry it with us.

Introducing dramatic conventions to 4-, 5- and 6-year-olds

By the time children are 4, 5 and 6 years, their drama work should have moved away from continuous 'plot making' to work that is more reflective. There should be, by the 5- and 6-year-old stage, a greater emphasis on the exploration of characters, motives and events. Children will need to be given names for the conventions they are using so that by working with the same ones frequently they become familiar with them and understand how to use, manipulate and communicate through them.

We can organize different aspects of meaning and highlight understanding by shaping the drama through the skilful use of these conventions. The same convention can be employed at different stages in the story to achieve different results. The use of hot seating, at the opening of a story, engaging the whole group and teacher in role, for example, might be used to set the scene, give information and plan action. The use of hot seating in the middle of an ongoing story may be used to look more closely at motives or as an investigation into certain actions or attitudes.

Picture books and stories offer endless possibilities, rich with potential. When working from a known story we may use dramatic conventions to:

- retell the story;
- explore significant moments in the story;
- extend the story;
- change the course of action in the story;
- fill in the gaps and explore what the text does not tell us.

With a new story we may use dramatic conventions to structure the children's predictions about the story. In each case we are working from a shared context, but allowing children the opportunity of individual interpretation. We have learned that children are not content to simply retell or re-enact known stories, but that they want to be creators with the ability to change, manipulate, complicate and extend them.

Initially, dramatic conventions can be introduced in conjunction with story time. After sharing the telling of a story, the children could work with one convention. They could make still images of different events from the story. The adult could adopt teacher in role as one of the characters from the story so that the children could interview and extend their understanding of that character and his or her motivations.

The following examples show some work undertaken with 4-year-olds who had shared the story of *Ruby* by Maggie Glen (1992). The bears have just escaped from the factory and 'they ran silently, swiftly through the night and into the day'. The children, in role as the bears from the factory, make still images of their escape. Miss T. uses thought-tracking to hear where the 'bears' are going. She touches children gently on the shoulder to indicate she wants them to speak:

Andrew:	I am running away to the shops.
Liam:	I'm going to hide in the beds.
Saiqa:	[Pause.]
Miss T:	Where are you going?
Saiqa:	To the shops.
Mark:	I'm going to the baker.
Chantelle:	I'm going somewhere to hide.

We suggest that an ideal way of showing children how to use hot seating is by interviewing a significant character. Miss T. used Kipper from *The Toys' Party* to introduce the convention to her group.

	[Sam, in role as Kipper, sits on a chair (the 'hot seat') and is asked questions by the other children.]
James:	Was your mum angry?
Kipper:	'cause I made a mess.
Mark:	What did you put in the cake?

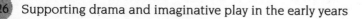

Kipper:	Jam, um, baked beans and milk. But the jam was for tea, so Mum was cross.
Chantelle:	Did you eat the cake?
Kipper:	Yes.
Miss T.:	How did it taste?
Kipper:	Not very nice. The toys didn't eat it, didn't want to.

The important thing to remember about dramatic conventions is that when they are used all children can be involved. It is possible with some conventions for all children to contribute at the same time (as in still images) but for each child to have an individual interpretation. Contrasting interpretations serve only to enrich the experience for all involved.

Application of dramatic conventions using 'Jack and the Beanstalk'

The following examples illustrate how to apply conventions using the story of 'Jack and the Beanstalk'. In this way we can see not only how conventions work in isolation, but also how they can be threaded together within a drama session.

Still images

A still image is a quick and simple convention. As its name suggests, it is concerned with the creation of a picture that does not move, using the body and face to communicate. We often explain it to children by telling them that we want them to hold their bodies still – to freeze as if posing for a photograph. The children are physically and visually representing a character or moment taken from a story they know or are making. They have to decide what they think or feel about this moment in time and communicate it.

This convention can involve working individually, in pairs or in groups. The child may be in role, as the pretend self, making the image, or it may be a personal response out of role. Images that are created in pairs or groups require the picture to become more complex. As we look at the interaction between characters or participants we can begin to observe children's understanding of what they are making.

Still images are often used in the initial stages of drama. Their effect is immediate and they enable us to focus the children and build their commitment to the drama, allowing them all to have an individual interpretation of a character or situation.

Example of work

To start a drama session all of the children, who have previously shared and discussed the story, make still images of Jack:

- Jack is hungry, as there is no food;
- Jack is going off to market with the cow (is he excited, worried, hungry or sad?);
- Jack swaps the cow for the beans (show how he feels about this: is he worried, excited?).

Still images are a good way for the adult to see if children have varying interpretations of a character. The convention is a very controlled way of communicating thoughts or opinions in one expression. It can be a useful strategy to return to throughout the drama, to focus on significant moments, such as the moment Jack shows his mum the beans, or the moment Jack opens his curtains and sees the beanstalk.

A still image can be a good way to introduce working in pairs. The children will have to share their ideas and negotiate the picture, but do not yet have the added complication of dialogue. The task remains tightly structured.

Example of work

In pairs as Jack and Jack's mum, make a still image of the moment Jack presents his mum with the beans. What does the picture tell us? How do we think she is going to respond?

This convention can be used as a control strategy for calming and refocusing the drama. It is also effective when used at the end of the drama to aid reflection. The children may be asked to make a still image of their ending to a story, allowing individual interpretation and a happy ending for those children who need a happy resolution. Children could also make still images of their favourite, happiest or saddest moments of the drama. When there is potential for violent or rapid action in a story, such as a chase or a fight, making a still image of the event can be a very effective controlling device.

Pointers

- Make sure the children are clear about the nature of the image and who/what they are representing.
- Although this convention can be undertaken instantly, the children need to be given a little time to think about their image or to discuss it if they are working in pairs/groups.
- If you think it would be of value, allow time to refine and re-present images, especially when children are new to the convention.
- Take time to share and interpret images, if appropriate to the drama. It can be valuable to see how children 'read' or interpret images made by others. It also adds value to the activity.
- Contrasting images can be used: initial perceptions, final perceptions, sad ending, happy ending.

Still images provide a good link to other conventions, such as thought-tracking and living pictures.

Thought-tracking

Thought-tracking is used when we want to ask children in role to speak the thoughts or feelings of a character at a particular given moment in time. It is often used in conjunction with still images. Having requested a still image the practitioner can then thought-track that image.

Example of work

The children have made a still-image of the moment Jack swaps the cow for the beans. Thought-track to find out how Jack feels about the swap. The children hold their images still and the adult explains that if they gently touch a child on the shoulder, that child should share what Jack is thinking or feeling at that moment. For example:

'I'm feeling happy';
'I don't want this nasty cow';
'I'm excited to plant my beans';
'I'm excited because I've got beans'.

The atmosphere is controlled and the children listen as others offer their contributions. The children may offer diverse comments and have the freedom to stray from the limitations of the text. The examples of comments made by children throughout this chapter are from reception children. In the examples above, all the children spoke in role. It may take some time to develop this. Initially children may present their still image and when they are thought-tracked say 'Jack is excited'.

During significant moments in a drama or during interactive story-making, the action may be frozen and characters thought-tracked to reveal their private thoughts and feelings. Again, this gives children an opportunity to individually interpret and represent a situation. Pausing the action and reflecting in this way deepens understanding of how people might feel in certain situations, explores motives and highlights how people can present contrasting inward and outward appearances. Thought-tracking encourages a sensitive response to the drama.

Example of work

Children, having been thought-tracked as Jack after he has been told off by his mum for swapping the cow for the beans, made these contributions:

'I feel sad';
'Just wait until my beanstalk grows!';
'I wish I didn't do it';
'I'll have to get that cow back!'

Pointers

- It is not compulsory for children to contribute. Silence ought be respected and children should know that they have a right to remain silent. We explain to the children that when they are touched on the shoulder we would like them, if they can, to tell a little of what this person is thinking or feeling at this moment in time. If there is no response, or there is a signal from the child to show us that they do not want to respond this time, then we simply move on, without the mood having been broken.
- This speaking of thoughts is not a performance and there is no correct response. The idea is not that all the children will repeat the same thoughts. A diversity of responses enriches the drama and promotes an understanding of the complexity of human behaviour.
- This convention can be used to examine the child's depth of involvement and thought in the drama.

Living pictures

This is another convention that works well from the starting point of a still image. The simplest way of explaining it is to say that living pictures bring still images to life. In pairs or small groups, still images focus on a moment in time. Living pictures introduce dialogue and add clarity and a deeper understanding of a situation. Living pictures can help us to understand interactions and relationships between characters.

Example of work

The children have worked in pairs to produce still-images showing the moment that Jack hands over the beans. When the teacher clicks her fingers all the children, in pairs, are to bring their pictures to life. What does Jack say? What does his mother say? This is done spontaneously for a very short time. One sentence each can be enough. The children can be given the opportunity to discuss their living picture and any changes they may wish to make, and then rerun their living picture. Children may wish to present their image and dialogue to the group, but this is not always necessary or productive.

Here's a typical exchange:

Mum: I don't want those beans, I'm going to throw them out of the window.

Jack: Oh Mum, I'm sorry for buying these beans.

Mum: You naughty little boy, you'll go to bed without no supper and no tea, you will have no tea for a week.

Jack: No.

Mum: You take those beans back.

Jack: No.

Mum: You'll have no supper.

Jack: I'll eat the beans then.

Pointers

- When you ask children to bring a picture to life it is often to explore a significant moment or to provide a snapshot of how characters interact. As such, it is better to let the action run for only a short time and then to freeze the picture again. The clicking of fingers to both start and stop the action can easily signal this.
- Allow the children time to reflect on their living picture, discuss it and repeat it.

- Use living pictures to share work. Ask pairs/groups who are willing to make their still image and bring it to life at the click of a finger.
- Again, there may be different interpretations of the same situation. Use this richness to question the children and understand their interpretations.
- Respect the children's contributions but do not be afraid to play with their ideas, particularly if you feel they may have misunderstood the focus of the work. We can value their contributions while at the same time enhancing their understanding.
- Have a clear focus about the living picture. What is significant about this moment that warrants it being brought to life? What will the value and learning be?

Teacher in role

As mentioned in previous chapters, this is the most powerful tool at the adult's disposal. To define teacher in role, we are talking about all the times within drama that the adult adopts role and behaves 'as if' they were someone other than themselves. When the adult does this, for whatever period of time, they are demonstrating their commitment to the drama, which in turn can help the children's commitment and bring integrity to the work. As explained earlier, the expectation is not that the adult is going to enter into some elaborate performance, but that they will behave with integrity in a role. They are speaking the words of someone other than themselves, in order to develop the story. It is an opportunity for the adult and children to put their usual roles and status to one side and interact in a new context. Teacher in role can be an influential way to give information, challenge perceptions, control, encourage involvement, develop the narrative and maximize on the learning potential of the drama.

Example of work

The teacher takes the role of the Giant from *Jack and the Beanstalk*. In preparing the children, she asks them what they expect the Giant to be like. They invariably have negative images of the Giant as 'fat', 'horrible', or 'angry'. The teacher explains that she is going to take on the role of the Giant and will signal moving in and out of role by using a simple item of clothing or a chair. She also reassures the children that this is safe and the Giant will not hurt anybody. When in role, the teacher provides a contrasting image of the Giant. He is lonely, misunderstood, big and awkward. He only wants to play with Jack; he has no friends. He would never hurt Jack and would love to come down the beanstalk, but is afraid of what would happen to him. This information gradually unfolds as the children ask questions and build a relationship with the Giant.

Pointers

- It is useful to use something that signals to the children when you are in and out of role. Whenever you adopt a role either sit on a special chair, or put on a simple item of clothing.
- Have a clear aim for adopting a role. Is it to introduce the drama, give information, provide a contrasting opinion, challenge thinking, or to refocus the drama?
- Think about the status of the role that you adopt and how it positions the children. For example, if you take on the low-status role of someone in need of help, the children are empowered into a high-status role where they have to guide and support you.
- Remember that at any point you have the option of stopping and coming out of role to control or clarify.
- Combine teacher in role with hot seating and encourage the children to question you in role. This is an excellent way of developing their questioning, speaking and listening skills.

Mantle of the expert

By manipulating the kinds of role we play we can place children in the role of the expert. When an adult takes on a low-status role and the children are required to be helpers and the solvers of problems we elevate their role into that of being the 'one who knows'. This changes the conventional classroom role of adults and children where the adult is always expected to be the expert.

Example of work

The adult takes on the role of Jack's mother and asks the children in role as Jack's friends to tell her about Jack and where he might have gone.

Pointers

- The children are usually placed in the position of experts – i.e. people with the specialist knowledge needed to complete a specific task. The specialist knowledge must be needed by the group to advance or inform the story.
- The teacher can learn about the children's perceptions of various roles within a community. The way children adopt the role of a parent, teacher, doctor etc. may reveal aspects of their real-life experiences of such people.

Hot seating

Hot seating allows the children, as themselves, to have the opportunity to question either an adult or one of their peers who is in a role connected to the drama or a story. This may take place at any point. At the start of a drama, hot seating can be used to gather information. During the drama, or at the end, it can be used to question characters about motivations, decisions and feelings.

Example of work

A child is in role as Jack, on the hot seat, and the other children question him about his first journey up the beanstalk. What did he find? How did he feel?

Pointers

- Children may need support in this role. One way of doing this is by preparing the children who are going to ask questions by asking *them* what questions it might be useful to ask – what do they want to find out, etc.? This way the child may have a more meaningful, productive experience. As the adult you can also provide support by asking questions that lead the children in the right direction, modelling appropriate, open questions. It may also be helpful to ease the child into the role by asking a few basic questions that do not rely on individual interpretation.
- After one child has successfully completed the hot seating it has been our experience that others will ask if they can have a go. Sometimes they may simply repeat what a peer has said, and at other times they may realize that they can control and change events. We think it is valuable to find time to let children play with a convention in this way. The

learning potential is rich and all children can participate in the questioning and develop their role as questioners.

A *sample lesson plan*

We have so far discussed the importance of introducing dramatic conventions gradually, so as to enable both adults and children to gain confidence and familiarity in using them, as well as an understanding of how they are best applied. Table 9.1 is an example of how dramatic conventions alone can be used to structure a drama lesson. We have taken isolated examples from 'Jack and the Beanstalk', and developed them into a lesson plan demonstrating how each drama strategy could be used.

Table 9.1 Jack and the Beanstalk: a drama session using dramatic conventions, suitable for children of 5 and 6 years.

Drama strategy	Procedure: what are the children going to do?	Procedure: what are you going to do?	Learning outcomes
Introducing the drama. Group discussion.	Sit in a circle and take part part in the discussion.	Sit children in a circle. Explain to the childen that they are going to be taking part in drama work about the story of 'Jack and the Beanstalk'. Define a space where the drama will take place. Remind the children of agreed ground rules/ contract making.	Children listen to others and make contributions. They develop skills in working cooperatively as part of a group.
Still image.	Children make a still image of Jack when he is hungry with no food.	Encourage children to think about how they are going to use their body to communicate. Work in a circle. Count to three and then ask all the children to produce their still image.	Children develop a personal response to a story. They engage in imaginary roles and use drama conventions to communicate meaning.

Table 9.1   (Continued)

Drama strategy	Procedure: what are the children going to do?	Procedure: what are you going to do?	Learning outcomes
Still image.	Children make a still image of Jack as he heads off to market with the cow. How is he feeling? Excited? Nervous? Sad?	Work to build commitment to the drama. Count to three and ask the children to produce their still image. Ask the children to hold their image very still, but to let their eyes move around the circle so that they can see the work of others.	
Still image.	Children make a still image of Jack the moment he swaps the beans for the cow. How is he feeling? Excited? Worried?	Count to three and ask the children to produce their still image. Again, let the children hold their image still while they let their eyes move around the circle to view the images made by other children.	
Still image and thought-tracking.	Children hold their previous still picture (Jack as he swaps the beans for the cow) while they are thought-tracked.	Explain to the children that you want to find out what Jack is thinking or feeling at this moment in time and if you touch them on the shoulder, maybe they can speak some words, as if they were Jack, to let us know what he is thinking or feeling (if children are silent, or do not want to contribute, that is accepted).	Children are able to identify with characters and actions and speak in role. They become aware that different points of view exist.

Table 9.1 (Continued)

Drama strategy	Procedure: what are the children going to do?	Procedure: what are you going to do?	Learning outcomes
Discussion.	Children discuss what happens when Jack returns home with the beans.	Guide the children through the discussion in order to prepare them for their next task. What happens when Jack gets home? Why is his mum angry? What do you think she might say to Jack? How might Jack feel?	Children explore and recall stories, understand characters, actions and motivations.
Still image (working with a partner).	Working with a partner, the children produce a still image as mum and Jack, showing the moment that Jack shows his mum the beans.	Give the children time to decide on which role they are taking and time briefly to discuss their image.	Children work cooperatively in pairs, using dramatic conventions to communicate about relationships.
Living pictures.	The children create the conversation between mum and Jack.	Explain that when you click your fingers you are going to bring the still-images to life, so that we can find out what mum said and what Jack said when he returned home and showed her the beans. To freeze the picture, click again.	Children work cooperatively speaking and interacting in role, identifying with and interpreting characters and actions, experimenting with language.

Table 9.1   (Continued)

Drama strategy	Procedure: what are the children going to do?	Procedure: what are you going to do?	Learning outcomes
Living pictures.	The children discuss their living picture out of role, talking about how they may change or refine it.	Explain that you are going to give the children a short time to talk about their living picture and any changes they may want to make, before asking them to repeat the still image and bring it to life again.	Children evaluate own work and work of others and suggest changes.
Living pictures, performance/ sharing of work, discussion.	Children take it in turns to share their work, if both partners are happy to do so.	Create a safe environment in which the children feel happy to share their work. Encourage children to listen to and appreciate the work of others. Draw children's attention to the differences between scenes. Discuss how characters feel.	Children present their work to an audience and appreciate the work of others. They develop awareness of the needs of an audience. They develop an understanding of different points of view and identify with the characters.
Still image.	Children make a still image of Jack the moment he opens his curtains and finds the beanstalk.	Refocus the children and move the drama on. Count to three and then ask the children to present their image, as before.	Children use dramatic conventions to communicate meaning.
Still image.	Children make a still image of Jack when he climbs the beanstalk for the first time.	Maintain commitment to the drama. Count to three as children present their images.	

Table 9.1   (Continued)

Drama strategy	Procedure: what are the children going to do?	Procedure: what are you going to do?	Learning outcomes
Still image and thought-tracking.	Children make a still image of Jack when he sees the Giant for the first time. They listen and contribute, as children are thought-tracked.	Guide the children through the still image. Ask them to hold images as you thought-track, to find out their responses to the Giant.	Children speak in role.
Discussion.	Children take part in a discussion about their perceptions of the Giant.	Facilitate the children's discussion about the Giant. Encourage words to describe the Giant. Explain that you are going to take on the role of the Giant.	Children listen and respond to others and use descriptive vocabulary.
Teacher in role.	Children, as themselves, question the Giant.	In role as the Giant, provide a conflicting view of him. He is lonely, misunderstood, big and awkward. He only wants to play with Jack but always frightens him by mistake and would love to have a friend but is too frightened to come down the beanstalk.	Children use their questioning skills. They explore simple social and moral issues and dilemmas. They begin to understand alternative points of view.
Discussion.	Discuss if the children should help the Giant and possibilities of how this could be done.	Lead discussion, listening to the children's interests and concerns. Discuss how the Giant's dilemma could be further explored next session; how the children would like to do that; and dramatic strategies they suggest using.	Children explore ideas, make decisions and suggest the use of appropriate dramatic forms.

Table 9.1   (Continued)

Drama strategy	Procedure: what are the children going to do?	Procedure: what are you going to do?	Learning outcomes
Reflection.	Children have the opportunity to share any comments about the drama session.	Allow the opportunity to share any comments about the drama session. Aspects the children liked or disliked, evaluation of their work or the work of others.	Children evaluate the drama process and contributions made by themselves and others.

Some stories that can be explored through the use of drama conventions

We are recommending some of the books we have used, not only because of their content, but also because they reflect a diversity of cultures and ethnic backgrounds.

Giant Hiccups by Jacqui Farley (1994) is about a friendly female giant called Ayesha. She lives at the bottom of a hill; many people who live and work there inhabit the top of the hill. One day, Ayesha has a problem with hiccups that make the town at the top of the hill tremble and shake. People think that it is an earthquake and run down the hill to escape. As they do so they come face to face with Ayesha. When they realize it is her hiccups that are the problem they set about finding ways of curing them.

The illustrations are beautiful and reflect a diversity of races. The giant is a female character who is portrayed as calm, friendly and peaceful. It is an excellent story for retelling or extending. The story explores problem solving and working together. What do people think when they feel the earth trembling but do not know why (thought-tracking)? What other ways could we find to cure Ayesha's hiccups (still-image and living pictures)? Does Ayesha mind that she is not part of the town community (hot seating)? How could the town's people welcome her to their community (living pictures)?

Finished Being Four by Verna Allette Wilkins (1992) reflects a diversity of cultures and we have used it to talk about birthdays and birthday parties. It is a useful book when working with children with special educational needs who need the safety of rituals and known experiences. Working alongside more able children, they can participate in still-images and living pictures.

I'll Take You to Mrs Cole by Nigel Gray and Michael Foreman (1987) has become a favourite. The central character is an African Caribbean boy who lives in fear of his neighbour, Mrs Cole. His mother has instilled the fear because she does not approve of Mrs Cole, who runs a messy and noisy house. It is a story about prejudice and how people make judgements on appearance. The boy overcomes his prejudice when he has to turn to Mrs Cole for support.

When using this story, it is useful to read only the first part to begin with. You can then make still-images of Mrs Cole, or make living pictures of what it is like inside her house. You can hot seat a child in role as the boy and find out what he thinks about Mrs Cole. Later the adult can take on a teacher in role as Mrs Cole to challenge the children's initial perceptions. They will soon find out she is kind and caring.

Conclusion

Many more dramatic conventions can be found in other books on drama that are not listed here. This is not to say that we think them unimportant, but we feel there are some that are unsuitable for very young children. We have found that young children, and the adults working with them, have successfully enjoyed the conventions we have outlined in this chapter. Young children need to be introduced to dramatic conventions gradually and those used should be practised frequently so that children can become familiar with them. Initially it is helpful to focus on the introduction of a single convention before combining conventions to create a longer drama lesson.

Summary

This chapter has:

- described the use of the following dramatic conventions: still-images, thought-tracking, living pictures, hot seating, teacher in role and mantle of the expert;
- discussed the need to introduce drama conventions to young children gradually;
- demonstrated how conventions can be used in isolation or as a complete drama session.

10

Observation, progression and assessment

Why observe?

Throughout this chapter we will be examining how we can use observation to evaluate and assess continuity, progression and provision. As parents, carers and practitioners, it is difficult to make time to observe our children. Days – for all of us – are busy, and in the case of practitioners the management of an ever-increasing curriculum is demanding. However, if we are putting time and dedication into planning the learning environment and learning opportunities for our children, it is essential that we also take the time to evaluate the results.

We will only know if the equipment we are providing is stimulating and challenging, or if the children are interacting in the role play area, by watching and keeping thorough records. The demands of daily life are resulting in less time to listen to children and match learning opportunities to their needs and interests. Most importantly, without careful observation we will not find out about children's immediate interests, questions and problems.

Observation is as important for parents at home as it is for practitioners in care and educational settings. Observing children can reveal their concerns. It was through observations in our role play area (a doctor's surgery), where a group of children were frequently exploring death, that we discovered that a girl in the class thought she was responsible for her grandfather's death. This was a burden she carried and it affected all areas of her learning. Only by listening to and observing children can we begin to provide learning relevant to the child and their world.

Ways of observing

There are many different ways of and different reasons for observing. It is useful to start with a personal research question and then plan into your day some time to observe and find answers to that question.

Questions may be about areas of provision:

- What is happening in the role play area? (Is the quality of play as you would expect? Are the children interacting, or just playing alongside each other? Do the children speak in role to each other? Do they create a story? Is the area well resourced, or are there arguments over clothing and props?)
- Who is playing in the role play area? (Are a variety of children using the role play area, or is it being dominated by a few? Are there children who never use the role play area? Why?)

We may have questions about individual children:

- Why doesn't Zara use the role play area? (Does she choose not to use the role play area, or is she restricted in some way? Does the content of the role- play area seem uninteresting or irrelevant to her? Does she know how to use the role play area? Might she need some adult support?)
- Why does Jack's cooperative play often end in confrontation? (Is Jack able to compromise or does he always have to have his own way? Do other children listen to him? Do other children find it hard to under-stand his speech impediment?)

Time sampling could be used to answer the above questions. Every ten minutes throughout the day, note down who is using the role play area. As well as answering specific questions, you will also find additional information, such as friendship patterns. Alternatively, you could observe the child at specific activities or in specific situations, either created by you, or that happen naturally.

It is important when using observations that we are clear about how we reach our conclusions. Are our conclusions drawn from what we see, or from our interpretation of what we see? If you have entered the role play area to find all its contents stacked in one corner you could interpret this as a disregard for and lack of care of property. However, it could be part of a wonderfully cooperative story about moving house. If you acted on your instant interpretation or imposed adult values of 'tidiness', you would have destroyed a sustained interactive learning experience that the children created and owned.

Similarly, we have known children to remain silent and seemingly passive throughout drama sessions. Later they have told us how much they enjoyed the drama, or made a comment that revealed their depth of involvement and understanding. It is important that we describe the context and the event rather than make a value judgement. We have to be clear about what we observe and realize that our interpretations and judgements may not be accurate or conclusive.

Observation is a powerful method of assessment. When we witness something, it tends to be ingrained in our memory. We are often surprised by our observations and understand anew the children in our care. It is important that all adults working in the setting are involved in observations and that observational techniques are shared with them. They are then attuned to observing children both formally and informally. Children often have special relationships with certain adults in the caring or educational setting. Every adult is an extra pair of eyes that needs to be used and valued.

You can collect evidence about children's learning in a variety of ways. By talking to children, in and out of role, and listening to them talking to each other, you can evaluate commitment and understanding of drama skills. Constant monitoring through discussion with others who work with you builds a wider picture of each child. You can set up activities through the use of dramatic conventions that provide diagnostic and formative information about progress. You need to decide how much evidence you require and how you are going to record it.

We need to be aware of the inhibiting factors related to observation and assessment identified by the Assessment Reform Group (1999: 5). They suggest that there is a tendency for teachers to assess quantity of work and presentation rather than the quality of learning, and that assessment is made difficult due to teachers not knowing enough about their pupils' learning needs.

Methods of observation during story-making and drama sessions

So far we have focused on observing children when they are working independently. When we are leading children in drama activities the use of observation becomes more complex because we are so involved in what is happening. It would certainly be difficult to focus on more than one or two children within a session. The use of other adults is of great importance. We have also found other useful methods of recording events for later analysis. For example:

- *Video.* This can be used after a session to watch a variety of children and can highlight aspects of the drama that you may not have noticed while facilitating it (it is also useful for observing your own practice!).

- *Tape-recording.* Again, this can help us remember children's questions and comments. A tape-recorder can be left to record in an area where children are working independently, such as work with puppets, play with small-world toys or storytelling in the sand. It is important to monitor outcomes.
- *Photographs.* A good visual reminder, photographs can also be shared with children, allowing them to reflect on their experience.
- *Recall/reflection.* Reflection is an important element of drama and comments that children offer in reflection can communicate their level of understanding. They should have opportunities to reflect not only on their experience, but to talk about the work of others too.
- *Presentation/sharing work.* When children present work, usually in an informal way, they share elements of their private process – their thinking and their response to a situation. We also have to be aware of what aspects of the work we are assessing, and not judge children solely on their presentation skills. There may also be children who feel uncomfortable sharing their work in this way.

What are we looking for?

Children should engage in drama to develop their skills, knowledge and understanding of drama, as a subject in its own right and as a method of making sense of the world. Both parents and practitioners should assess their children's progress in relation to this. In educational settings, drama can be used to support work in a variety of curriculum areas. We may therefore need to assess in relation to subject-specific criteria.

A framework for learning

Drama skills and knowledge

Children should have opportunities to create, participate in and respond to drama. In creating and participating in drama, children should have opportunities to:

- engage in imaginary play, roles and situations;
- explore and understand the difference between pretend and reality;
- interact with roles adopted by others, including adults;
- communicate meaning by using their bodies, space, movement and language, in a variety of contexts;
- explore ideas and stories;

- create stories;
- communicate by presenting their work;
- begin to use drama conventions to communicate meaning.

In responding to drama, children should have opportunities to:

- reflect on their drama experiences;
- remember and recall dramatic action;
- identify with characters and actions;
- evaluate contributions made by themselves and others;
- suggest the use of appropriate dramatic conventions;
- see live performances by peers, the wider school, the community and professional companies.

In terms of personal and social skills, drama should offer opportunities to develop:

- self-confidence and social confidence;
- their experience of roles that reach beyond the child's self;
- speaking and listening skills;
- a sense of enquiry;
- skills in working cooperatively in a group or with a partner;
- personal views and opinions;
- an awareness of different points of view;
- an understanding of moral and social issues;
- an understanding of cause and consequence.

Provision and progression in drama

It is possible to identify progression in drama, although across the age ranges we are continually developing and reinforcing what has gone before, rather than moving through a strict sequence of progression. We are working to the same broad aim – to develop the child's ability to use drama form. There are many aspects to consider when planning for drama, such as children's development of cognitive and social skills, and their previous experiences of drama. This will affect where we begin and our aims for the progression. Therefore, the progression outlined below should be used only as a guide, and matched appropriately to children's needs.

Provision for children of 1–3 years
This age group should have opportunities to:

- work in role play areas;

- use dressing-up clothes;
- work with small-world/-play people (including use in sand and water areas);
- hear storytelling from adults (oral and from books; stories supported by puppets and artefacts);
- work with resources for enacting/re-enacting stories;
- take part in interactive storytelling;
- work with puppets;
- learn action songs and rhymes;
- take part in spontaneous dramatic/imaginary play (with teacher support and teacher in role);
- experience adults using teacher in role;
- make dens (inside and outside);
- see live performances by peers, the wider school, the community and professional companies.

Progression for children of 1–3 years
This age group should:

- use scenarios from their everyday experiences in their dramatic play, such as cooking food or feeding the baby;
- adopt roles that they see around them;
- use objects with similar characteristics to represent other objects;
- start to introduce a storyline to their play;
- play alongside other children, connected by a theme (e.g. doctors);
- begin to work cooperatively within a group, with adult support;
- respond to teacher in role (can be used in various contexts from introducing a character from a story to posing dilemmas in the role play area);
- create stories with adult support (use varied provision, role play area, puppets, small world, construction, sand- and water-tray);
- retell stories with adult support;
- take part in interactive storytelling (working in various-sized groups and various locations, making contributions and listening to the contributions of others, becoming aware of mood, tension and feelings);
- use simplified dramatic conventions when appropriate;
- recall aspects of the stories they have helped to create;*
- talk about aspects of their drama experiences they have liked and disliked;*
- talk about characters from stories read and created;*
- talk about performances they have seen, including likes and dislikes.

* in a small group with other children and adult support.

Provision for children of 4–5 years
This age group should have opportunities to:

- work in role play areas;
- use dressing-up clothes;
- work with small-world/-play people (including use in sand and water areas);
- hear storytelling from adults (oral and from books; stories supported by puppets and artefacts);
- work with resources for enacting/re-enacting stories;
- take part in interactive storytelling;
- work with puppets;
- learn action songs and rhymes;
- take part in spontaneous dramatic/imaginary play (with teacher support and teacher in role);
- use dramatic conventions for individual, small-group, whole-group and paired work;
- see live performances by peers, the wider school, the community and professional companies.

Progression for children of 4–5 years
This age group should:

- develop their use of narrative and storylines in their play;
- revisit narratives and themes and increase complexity;
- extend the roles they adopt to include wider influences, such as characters from books and television;
- use objects with no shared characteristics to represent other objects;
- begin to work cooperatively and independently;
- accept and interact with the teacher's use of role;
- create and retell stories independently and with adult support (the adult works with the children to extend narrative, clarity and understanding; there should be a balance between independent and adult-supported work);
- take part in interactive storytelling (the children are at a stage where their main interest is to create the plot and it is important that we give them opportunities to indulge and experiment with this; the children are able to work in a whole class group, they make decisions and solve problems, developing their understanding of cause and consequence);
- gradually introduce dramatic conventions (still image, thought-tracking, living pictures, hot seating);
- begin to use conventions to communicate meaning (becoming aware of

how to use their bodies, space and movement to communicate; able to speak in role to adults and other children);
- use dramatic conventions to explore stories;
- work in pairs, small groups and as a class;
- present their work to others (limited awareness of audience needs and communicating with audience);
- begin to evaluate and appreciate their work and the work of others (able to identify what were for them important moments);
- begin to identify with characters and actions;
- become aware that different points of view exist;
- explore simple moral and social issues.

Provision for children of 5–6 years
This age group should have opportunities to:

- work in role play areas;
- use dressing-up clothes;
- work with small-world/-play people (including use in sand and water areas);
- hear storytelling from adults (oral and from books; stories supported by puppets and artefacts);
- work with resources for enacting/re-enacting stories;
- take part in interactive storytelling;
- work with puppets;
- learn action songs and rhymes;
- take part in spontaneous dramatic/imaginary play (with teacher support and teacher in role);
- use dramatic conventions for individual, small-group, whole-group and paired work;
- present short performances to peers/parents (e.g. during assembly);
- see live performances by peers, the wider school, the community and professional companies;
- work with simple play scripts.

Progression for children of 5–6 years
This age group should:

- create more complex narratives, with a wide range of characters and action;
- mime missing props;
- work independently in a cooperative manner;
- create and retell stories independently and share short scenes with others;
- take part in the exploration of stories (they are more able to cope with

the action being stopped and started; adults introduce the use of dramatic conventions to explore the storytelling, the children listen and respond to the ideas of others and negotiate with others about the direction of the drama);

- use dramatic conventions to explore stories and contexts (children make suggestions about which conventions could be used; they can sustain role for a longer period, and interact in role with other children and adults; they are more aware of how to use space, movement, language and their bodies to communicate);
- work individually, in pairs, small groups and as a whole class (they are more able to work cooperatively, developing personal views and learning to respect the views of others; they are developing sensitivity when exploring moral and social issues);
- present their work to others (with a growing awareness of audience and the need to communicate with the audience);
- evaluate and appreciate their work and the work of others, including live performance (children talk about significant moments in the drama, suggest ways in which the drama might continue, suggest drama forms/conventions that might be used; they identify with characters and actions and can talk about cause and consequence);
- begin to explore simple scripts (children explore how dramatic action can be recorded and compare the use of scripts to creating their own drama; they may produce short extracts of script from their own drama experiences).

A comprehensive list of progression for 4-, 5- and 6-year-old children is provided under the drama strand of the QCA document *Teaching Speaking and Listening at Key Stages 1 and 2* (1999).

Conclusion

Monitoring children's progress is an important feature of the learning process. Deciding on which method to use and how often to use it is an important aspect of your planning and assessment.

A single observation or a single piece of work gathered from a drama session will not give an accurate picture of a child or a group of children. It takes time to build up a profile of what each child knows and understands and the skills they are developing. It is sometimes difficult to make judgements about progress on observations alone; talking on a regular basis with children and with your colleagues will establish a more accurate account of progress.

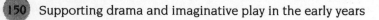

Summary

This chapter has examined:

- the need for consistent observation and non-judgemental assessment;
- the use of a variety of monitoring techniques;
- adequate provision for drama activity that leads to progression in drama skills.

Final thoughts

> In using drama as a teaching strategy, we need to create an environment in which talk is normal and desired, and in which the students' contributions are valued not only by the teacher but by their classmates. Both confidence and competence in their language abilities can be enriched and increased through the synthesis of language, feeling and thought.
>
> (Wagner 1998: 70–1)

Throughout this book we have highlighted the importance of 'the synthesis of language, feeling and thought'. The significance of talk and the development of oral language in the early years has been a major feature of the text. To build strong thinking skills and to increase cognitive and affective development, children need to experience activities that encourage their *oral* language abilities. We see the move towards the formality of reading and writing at the expense of developing talk as very detrimental to the intellectual growth of young children.

Through its immediacy, drama has the potential to engage children (especially young children) in different kinds of talk and contrasting forms of thinking. The future will require people who not only can think in a logical, sequential and systematic way (Bruner's paradigmatic thought), but people who can think in the world of dreams. This can only be realized if there has been enough room in early education for good quality pretend play and playfulness – not only on the part of children, but of adults as well.

We have tried to establish the importance of the use of pretend play in cognitive and emotional development. Using this innate ability to move from reality into the 'as if' allows us, the practitioners, to harness this aptitude for our own ends.

Drama in the early years should not be seen as an optional extra but as a crucial learning tool which develops the whole child. It helps children, among other things, to take ownership of their own learning, understand how other people behave and achieve insight into social interaction. As Epstein (1995: 63) reminds us 'children do not have completely free choices about the ways they behave or the people they become but they are, nonetheless, active agents in their own self-creation'.

We hope readers of this book, through a greater understanding of pretend play, will find the confidence to make all aspects of dramatic activity an integral part of their care and development of children. We hope the positive examples we have included will help the management of drama within the home, playgroup and nursery setting, and in school environments.

Bibliography

Aitcheson, J. (1997) *The Articulate Mammal*. London: Hutchinson.

Anning, A. and Edwards, A. (1999) *Promoting Children's Learning from Birth to Five*. Buckingham: Open University Press.

Assessment Reform Group (1999) *Assessment for Learning: Beyond the Black Box*. Cambridge: University of Cambridge School of Education.

Baldwin, P. and Hendy, L. (1994) *The Drama Book*. London: HarperCollins Educational.

Beardsley, G. (1998) *Exploring Play in the Primary Classroom*. London: David Fulton.

Bennett, N., Wood, L. and Rogers, S. (1996) *Teaching Through Play: Teachers' Theories and Classroom Practice*. Buckingham: Open University Press.

Bettleheim, B. (1975) *The Uses of Enchantment: The Meaning and Importance of Fairy Tales*. Harmondsworth: Penguin.

Bloom, B. and Krathwohl, D. (1965) *The Taxonomy of Educational Objectives: The Classification of Educational Goals*. London: Longman.

Bolton, G. (1984) *Drama as Education*. London: Longman.

Bolton, G. (1993) Drama in education and TIE: a comparison, in T. Jackson (ed.) *Learning Through Theatre*. London: Routledge.

Bolton, G. (1999) *Acting in Classroom Drama: A Critical Analysis*. Stoke-on-Trent: Trentham Books.

Booth, D. (1994) *Story Drama*. Ontario: Pembroke Publishers.

Bowlby, J. (1980) *Attachment and Loss: Loss, Sadness and Depression*. New York: Basic Books.

Bruce, T. (1991) *Time to Play in Early Childhood Education*. London: Hodder & Stoughton.

Bruner, J. (1986) *Actual Minds, Possible Worlds*. Cambridge, MA: Harvard University Press.

Burke, J. (2000) Toddlers go from the pram to the couch, *Observer*, 10 September.

Butterworth, N. (1992) *After the Storm*. London: Collins.

Claxton, G. (2000) A sure start for an uncertain world. *Early Education*, Spring.

Costello, P. (2000) *Thinking Skills and Early Childhood Education*. London: David Fulton.

Craft, A. (2000) *Creativity across Primary Education*. London: Routledge.

Curry, N. and Arnaud, S. (1984) Play in developmental pre-school settings, in T.D. Yawkey and A.D. Pelligrini (eds) *Child's Play: Developmental and Applied*. Hillsdale, NJ: Lawrence Erlbaum Associates.

David, T. (1999) *Young Children Learning*. London: Paul Chapman Publishing.

DfEE/QCA (Department for Education and Employment/Qualifications and Curriculum Authority) (1999a) *Early Learning Goals*. Sudbury: DfEE.

DfEE/QCA (Department for Education and Employment/Qualifications and Curriculum Authority) (1999b) *The National Curriculum: Handbook for Primary Teachers in England, Key Stages 1 and 2*. London: DfEE/QCA.

DfEE/QCA (Department for Education and Employment/Qualifications and Curriculum Authority) (2000a) *Early Years: Curriculum for Under-fives: Conference Report*. Sudbury: DfEE.

DfEE/QCA (Department for Education and Employment/Qualifications and Curriculum Authority) (2000b) *Curriculum Guidance for the Foundation Stage*. Sudbury: DfEE.

DfEE/SCAA (Department for Education and Employment/School Curriculum and Assessment Authority) (1996) *Nursery Education: Desirable Outcomes for Children's Learning on Entering Compulsory Education*. London: DfEE.

Dixon, J. (1991) Oral exchange: a historical review of the developing frame, in M. Maclure, T. Phillips and A. Wilkinson (eds) *Oracy Matters*. Buckingham: Open University Press.

Dunbar, J. (1990) *Five Mice and the Moon*. London: Orchard Books.

Dunn, J. (1988) *The Beginnings of Social Understanding*. Oxford: Blackwell.

Dunn, J. and Kendrick, C-A. (1982) *Siblings*. London: Grant McIntyre.

Edmonson, M.E. (1971) *Lore: An Introduction to the Science of Folklore and Literature*. New York: Holt, Rinehart & Winston.

Emihovich, C.A. (1980) Social interaction in two integrated kindergartens. *Integrated Education*, 19(3–6): 73.

Epstein, D. (1995) 'Girls don't do bricks': gender and sexuality in the primary classroom, in J. Siraj-Blatchford and I. Siraj-Blatchford (eds) *Educating the Whole Child: Cross-curricular Skills, Themes, and Dimensions*. Buckingham: Open University Press.

Farley, J. (1994) *Giant Hiccups*, illust. P. Venus. Singapore: Tamarind Books.

Fein, G. (1984) The self-building potential of pretend play, in T.D. Yawkey, and A.D. Pelligrini (eds) *Child's Play: Developmental and Applied*. Hillsdale, NJ: Lawrence Erlbaum Associates.

Fisher, R. (1990) *Teaching Children to Think*. Oxford: Blackwell.

Fox, C. (1993) *At the Very Edge of the Forest: the Influence of Literature on Storytelling by Children*. London: Cassell.

Furth, H.G. and Kane, S.R. (1992) Children constructing society: a new perspective on children's play, in H. McGurk (ed.) *Childhood social development*. London: LEA.

Garvey, C. (1977) *Play*. London: Fontana.

Glen, M. (1992) *Ruby*. London: Red Fox/Random House.

Goldman, L.R. (1998) *Child's Play: Myth, Memesis and Make-Believe*. Oxford: Berg.

Goleman, D. (1996) *Emotional Intelligence*. London: Bloomsbury.

Grainger, T. (1997) *Traditional Storytelling in the Primary Classroom*. Leamington Spa: Scholastic.

Gray, N. and Foreman, M. (1987) *I'll Take You to Mrs Cole*. London: Macmillan.

Guildford, J.P. (1958) Traits of creativity, in P.E. Vernon (ed.) *Creativity*. Harmondsworth: Penguin.

Halliday, M.A.K. (1975) Learning How to Mean – Explorations in the Development of Language. London: Edward Arnold.

Hammond, J. (2000) 'An investigation into role-play areas', unpublished PGCE research paper. University of Cambridge Faculty of Education.

Harris, P.L. and Kavanaugh, R.D. (1993) *Young Children's Understanding of Pretense*, monographs of the Society for Research in Child Development, vol. 58, no. 1. Chicago: University of Chicago Press.

Honig, A.S. (1983) Sex role and socialization in early childhood. *Young Children*, 38(6): 27–70.

Hornbrook D. (1991) *Drama in Education*. London: Falmer Press.

Hughes, M. and Cousins, J. (1991) The roots of oracy: early language at home and at school, in M. Maclure, T. Phillips and A. Wilkinson (eds) *Oracy Matters*. Buckingham: Open University Press.

Hurst, V. and Joseph, J. (1998) *Supporting Early Learning – The Way Forward*. Buckingham: Open University Press.

Hutt, S.J., Tyler, S., Hutt, C. and Christopherson, H. (1989) *Play, Exploration and Learning: A Natural history of Pre-school*. London: Routledge.

Jago, M. (1999) Bilingual children in a monolingual society, in T. David (ed.) *Young Children Learning*. London: Paul Chapman Publishing.

Jennings, S. (1999) *Introduction to Developmental Playtherapy: Playing and Health*. London: Jessica Kingsley.

Kenny, A. (1989) *The Metaphysics of the Mind*. Oxford: Oxford University Press.

Kempe, A. (1996) *Drama Education and Special Needs*. London: Stanley Thorne.

Kitson, N. (1994) 'Please Miss Alexander: will you be the robber?' Fantasy play: a case for adult intervention, in J. Moyles (ed.) *The Excellence of Play*. Buckingham: Open University Press.

Kitson, N. and Spivey, I. (1997) *Drama 7–11*. London: Routledge.

Leslie, A.M. (1987) Pretense and representation: the origins of 'theory of mind'. *Psychological Review*, 94: 412–26.

Levitt, E. and Cohen, S. (1976) Attitudes of children towards their handicapped peers. *Childhood Education*, 52: 171–3.

Mills, C. and Mills, D. (1998) *Dispatches: The Early Years*. London: Channel 4 Television.

Moreno, J.L. (1953) *Who Shall Survive? Foundations of Sociometry, Group Psycho-therapy and Sociodrama*. New York: Beacon House.

Morgan, N. and Saxton, J. (1987) *Teaching Drama*. London: Hutchinson.

Morgan, N. and Saxton, J. (1991) *Teaching, Questioning and Learning*. London: Routledge.

National Advisory Committee on Creative and Cultural Education (1999) *All Our Futures: Creativity, Culture and Education*. Sudbury: DfEE.

Neelands, J. (1992) *Learning Through Imagined Experience*. London: Hodder & Stoughton.

Nicholls, J. (1985) *'Magic Mirror' and Other Poems for Children*. London: Faber & Faber.

Nicholson, H. (1996) Voices on stage, in M. Styles, E. Bearne and V. Watson (eds) *Voices Off*. London: Cassell.

O'Connell, B. and Bretherton, I. (1984) Toddlers' play, alone and with mother: the role of maternal guidance, in I. Bretherton (ed.) *Symbolic Play: The Development of Social Understanding*. New York: Academic.

Ofsted (Office for Standards in Education) (1994) *First Class*. London: HMSO.

Ofsted (Office for Standards in Education) (2000) *The Annual Report of Her Majesty's Inspector of Schools*. London: The Stationery Office.

O'Neill, C. (1995) *Drama Worlds*. London: Heinemann.

Ong, W. (1987) *Orality and Literacy: The Technologizing of the World*. London: Methuen.

O'Toole, J. (1992) *The Process of Drama*. London: Routledge.

Parker-Rees, R. (1999) Protecting playfulness, in L. Abbott and H. Moylett (eds) *Early Education Transformed*. London: Falmer Press.

Piaget, J. (1952) *Play, Dreams and Imitation in Childhood*. London: Routledge.

Pinker, S. (1994) *The Language Instinct*. New York: William Morrow & Company.

Policastro, E. and Gardner, H. (1999) Case studies to robust generalisations, in R.J. Sternberg (ed.) *Handbook of Creativity*. Cambridge: Cambridge University Press.

QCA (Qualifications and Curriculum Authority) (1999) *Teaching Speaking and Listening in Key Stages 1 and 2*. Sudbury: QCA Publications.

Readman, G. and Lamont, G. (1994) *Drama: Handbook for Primary Teachers*. London: BBC Educational Publishing.

Roopnarine, J. (1984) Sex-typed socialization in mixed age pre-school children. *Child Development*, 55: 1078–84.

Rosen, H. (1991) The irrepressible genre, in M. Maclure, T. Phillips and A. Wilkinson (eds) *Oracy Matters*. Buckingham: Open University Press.

SCAA (School Curriculum and Assessment Authority) (1996) *Desirable Outcomes for Children's Learning on Entering Compulsory Education*. Sudbury: DfEE.

SCAA (School Curriculum and Assessment Authority) (1997) *Looking at Children's Learning*. Sudbury: DfEE.

Sealey, A. (1996) *Learning about Language*. Buckingham: Open University Press.

Sevinc, M. (1999) Symbolic play among Turkish pre-school children. Paper presented at 'Sharing Research in Early Childhood Education', third Warwick International Early Years Conference, April.

Singer, D. and Singer, J. (1990) *The House of Make-believe: Children's Play and the Developing Imagination*. Cambridge, MA: Harvard University Press.

Siraj-Blatchford, I. (1993) *The Early Years: Laying the Foundations for Racial Equality*. London: Trentham Books.

Slade, P. (1954) *Child Drama*. London: University of London Press.

Smilansky, S. (1968) *The Effects of Socio-dramatic Play on Disadvantaged Pre-School Children*. New York: Wiley.

Smilansky, S. and Shefatya, L. (1990) *Facilitating Play: A Medium for Promoting Cognitive, Socio-emotional and Academic Development in Young Children*. Gaithersburg, MD: Psychosocial and Educational Publications.

Smith, F. (1992) *To Think in Language, Learning and Education*. London: Routledge.

Smith, P.K. (1994) Play and the cues of play, in J. Moyles (ed.) *The Excellence of Play*. Buckingham: Open University Press.

Smith, P.K., Dalgleish, M. and Hertzmark, G. (1981) A comparison of the effects of fantasy play tutoring and skills tutoring in nursery classes. *International Journal of Behavioural Development*, 4: 421–41.

Snape, J. and Snape, C. (1989) *Giant*. London: Walker Books.

Souhami, J. (1998) *Rama and the Demon King*. London: Frances Lincoln.

Sparks Linfield, R. and Warwick, P. (1996) 'Do you know what MY name is?' Assessment in the early years: some examples from science, in D. Whitebread (ed.) *Teaching and Learning in the Early Years*. London: Routledge.

Sperber, D. and Wilson, D. (1987) *Relevance: Communication and Cognition*. Oxford: Blackwell.

Sylva, K., Roy, C. and Painter, M. (1980) *Childwatching at Playgroup and Nursery School*. London: Grant McIntyre.

Tizard, B. and Hughes, M. (1984) *Young Children Learning*. London: Fontana.

Toye, N. and Prendiville, F. (2000) *Drama and Traditional Story for the Early Years*. London: Routledge.

Van Ments, M. (1994) *The Effective Use of Role-play*. London: Kogan Page.

Vygotsky, L. (1978) *Mind in Society: Development of Higher Psychological Processes*. Cambridge, MA: Harvard University Press.

Wagner, B. (1979) *Dorothy Heathcote: Drama as a Learning Medium*. London: Hutchinson.

Wagner, B (1998) *Educational Drama and Language Arts*. Portsmouth, NH: Heinemann.

Way, B. (1967) *Development Through Drama*. London: Longman.

Wilkins, V.A. (1992) *Finished Being Four*. Singapore: Tamarind Books.

Wilkinson, A. (1965) *Spoken English (Educational Review* occasional publications no. 2). Birmingham: University of Birmingham School of Education.

Winnicott, D.W. (1971) *Playing and Reality*. Harmondsworth: Pelican Books.

Winston, J. (1998) *Drama, Narrative and Moral Education*. London: Falmer Press.

Index

149518